WORKBOOK
with Digital Pack

2

CEFR
B1

AMERICAN TH!NK

SECOND EDITION

Herbert Puchta,
Jeff Stranks &
Peter Lewis-Jones
with Clare Kennedy

ACKNOWLEDGEMENTS

Acknowledgements

The authors and publishers acknowledge the following sources of copyright material and are grateful for the permissions granted. While every effort has been made, it has not always been possible to identify the sources of all the material used, or to trace all copyright holders. If any omissions are brought to our notice, we will be happy to include the appropriate acknowledgements on reprinting and in the next update to the digital edition, as applicable.

Key: U = Unit.

Text

U6: Text about Greta Thunberg. Reproduced with kind permission of Connor Turner; **U11**: Text about 'Positive News magazine'. Reproduced with kind permission of Positive News; Text about 'The Happy Newspaper'. Reproduced with kind permission of The Happy Newspaper.

Photography

All the photographs are sourced from Getty Images.

U0: Jose Luis Pelaez Inc/DigitalVision; Louis Turner/Cultura; **U1:** Jef De Puydt/500px; Ariel Skelley/The Image Bank; SDI Productions/E+; Maskot; JB Lacroix/WireImage; **U2:** elenaleonova/E+; Andreas Speich/EyeEm; Gabriele Grassl/iStock/Getty Images Plus; csy302/iStock/Getty Images Plus; Photo by Bhaskar Dutta/Moment; gldburger/iStock/Getty Images Plus; GIPhotoStock/Cultura; Valerie Loiseleux/E+; biriberg/E+; Abdul Mukmin Abdullah/EyeEm; frentusha/iStock/Getty Images Plus; Vladimir Godnik; ciricvelibor/E+; SDI Productions/E+; mediaphotos/iStock/Getty Images Plus; PeopleImages/E+; Letizia Le Fur/ONOKY; Klaus Vedfelt/DigitalVision; **U3**: Caiaimage; kali9/E+; AntonioGuillem/iStock/Getty Images Plus; filo/E+; luismmolina/E+; ISerg/iStock/Getty Images Plus; Zoonar RF; 4x6/DigitalVision Vectors; Prakasit Khuansuwan/EyeEm; **U4:** Robert Daly/OJO Images; franz12/iStock/Getty Images Plus; domin_domin/E+; Yobro10/iStock/Getty Images Plus; Bloom Productions/Stone; JBryson/iStock/Getty Images Plus; Juanmonino/E+; Juanmonino/iStock/Getty Images Plus; H. Armstrong Roberts/Retrofile RF; **U5:** Dorling Kindersley/Getty Images; RapidEye/E+; sdigital/iStock/Getty Images Plus; adventtr/iStock/Getty Images Plus; J-Elgaard/iStock/Getty Images Plus; Suljo/iStock/Getty Images Plus; Nerthuz/iStock/Getty Images Plus; Tetra Images; shironosov/iStock/Getty Images Plus; momcilog/E+; Hero Images; Mark Horton/WireImage; Amanda Edwards/WireImage; William Perugini/Image Source; **U6:** rmitsch/E+; KEENPRESS/Stone; On-Air/iStock/Getty Images Plus; Peter Dazeley/Photographer's Choice RF; Spencer Platt/Getty Images News; Kristian Bell/Moment; urbazon/E+; whitemay/E+; James Emmerson/robertharding; Caspar Benson; Ignacio Palacios/Stone; South China Morning Post; **U7:** Flashpop/DigitalVision; Carol Yepes/Moment; gilaxia/iStock/Getty Images Plus; Pisan Kumpree/iStock/Getty Images Plus; Sandy Jones/Photodisc; Todd Ryburn Photography/Moment; Westend61; Hero Images; **U8:** BirdHunter591/iStock/Getty Images Plus; Ayaka Ihara/EyeEm; Tsuneo Yamashita/The Image Bank; Renate Hoffmann/EyeEm; buzbuzzer/E+; Jürgen Hüls/EyeEm; Image Source; Gabe Ginsberg/Getty Images Entertainment; **U9:** ZU_09/DigitalVision Vectors; Grove Pashley/Photographer's Choice; skynesher/E+; Mlenny/E+; Photonostop RM; MassanPH/Moment; Kentaroo Tryman/Maskot; Mikolette/E+; **U10:** Jacobs Stock Photography Ltd/DigitalVision; Westend61; Juice Images RF; Goodboy Picture Company/iStock/Getty Images Plus; Cavan Images; Eric Audras/ONOKY; ViewStock; Tetra Images; Halfpoint Images/Moment; **U11:** Plume Creative/DigitalVision; JTPalacio/Moment; **U12:** Maskot; Antenna; Thanit Weerawan/Moment; Ariel Skelley/DigitalVision; Bruno De Hogues/Photolibrary/Getty Images Plus; Awl Images RM.

Cover photographs by: David Sacks/The Image Bank/Getty Images; Alex Tihonov/Moment Open/Getty Images

The following photographs are sourced from other sources/libraries.

U11: Courtesy of Positive News; Courtesy of The Happy Newspaper; **U12:** JollyPopLA/Shutterstock; Courtesy of FoodCycle.

Illustrations

Dusan Lakicevic (Beehive Illustration) pp. 5, 15, 46, 74, 78, 86, 95; Adam Linley (Beehive Illustration) pp. 21, 42, 64, 75, 113; Mark Ruffle pp. 4, 17, 73, 80, 108, 114; Ben Scruton (Meiklejohn) pp. 10, 29, 37, 54, 75, 90; Szilvia Szakall (Beehive Illustration) pp. 8, 34, 72.

Grammar Rap video stills: Silversun Media Group.

Audio

Audio Produced by City Vox, New York.

CONTENTS

WELCOME

A GETTING TO KNOW YOU
Asking questions

1 Put the words in order to make questions.

0 are / from / where / you
Where are you from _____ ?

1 you / 15 / are
_____ ?

2 doing / you / are / what
_____ ?

3 do / do / you / what
_____ ?

4 do / like / doing / you / what
_____ ?

5 like / you / TV / watching / do
_____ ?

2 Write the right question from Exercise 1 for each answer.

0 A *Are you 15* _____ ?
B Yes, I am. Last Saturday was my 15th birthday.

1 A _____ ?
B I'm just finishing my homework. I won't be long.

2 A _____ ?
B Canada, but I live in the US.

3 A _____ ?
B Yes, I do, especially reality shows.

4 A _____ ?
B Hanging out with my friends. That's my favorite thing.

5 A _____ ?
B I'm a dentist.

3 Answer the questions in Exercise 1 so that they are true for you.

_____
_____
_____
_____
_____
_____
_____
_____
_____
_____

The weather

4 Match the pictures with the sentences.

0 It's dry and cloudy. [F]
1 It's warm and sunny. [ ]
2 It's cold and foggy. [ ]
3 It's hot and humid. [ ]
4 It's wet and windy. [ ]
5 It's rainy and freezing. [ ]

Families

5 Complete the sentences with the words in the list.

aunt | cousin | father | grandma | grandpa
husband | mother | sister | uncle | ~~wife~~

0 My mother is my father's _____ *wife* _____ .
1 My _____ is my mother's mother.
2 My _____ is my aunt's child.
3 My uncle is my aunt's _____ .
4 My aunt is my cousin's _____ .
5 My aunt is my father's _____ .
6 My _____ is my grandmother's husband.
7 My _____ is my cousin's father.
8 My _____ is my mother's husband.
9 My mother's sister is my _____ .

6 🔊 **W.01** **Listen and complete the table.**

	Relation to Zoe	Age	Nationality	Job
Jess				*student*
Mike				
Karen				

7 **Choose three people from your family. Write one or two sentences about each one.**

My aunt's name is Laura. She's from Brasilia.
She's 34 and she's a businesswoman.
_____
_____
_____
_____
_____
_____

SUMMING UP

8 Ⓒircle **the correct words.**

A Hey, what ⁰*you are /* *are you* doing?

B I'm writing an email to my ¹*cousin / brother* Lucy in Argentina.

A In Argentina? What ²*does she do / is she doing* there? Is she there on vacation?

B Yes. Her mother – my ³*aunt / uncle* – is from Argentina. They're there on vacation, visiting her family.

A That's nice. Is the weather good there right now?

B Yes, Lucy said it was ⁴*hot and sunny / freezing.*

A Hot? But it's January!

B In Argentina, January is summer, remember?

A Oh, right. Listen. ⁵*Are you / Do you* going to the movies tonight?

B No, why?

A There's a great movie out right now. Come and see it with us!

B OK, thanks. But I'll finish my email first!

B EXPERIENCES
Meeting people (tense review)

1 **Match the pictures with the sentences.**

1 She's met a lot of famous people. ☐

2 She met a famous actor last night. ☐

3 She was having dinner with an actor when her phone rang. ☐

2 **Complete the sentences. Use** *he* **and the verb** *eat* **in the tenses in parentheses.**

0 ____*He ate*____ a really good pizza last night. (simple past positive)

1 _____ any breakfast this morning. (simple past negative)

2 A _____ all his vegetables? (simple past question)

B _____ (negative short answer)

3 _____ when I called him. (past continuous statement)

4 A _____ Japanese food? (present perfect question with *ever*)

B _____ (positive short answer)

3 **Complete the sentences with the correct forms of the verbs.**

A Have you ever ⁰____*been*____ (be) late for a concert?

B Yes. I ¹_____ (be) late for a big concert last year. It was Ariana Grande.

A What ²_____ (happen)?

B Well, I ³_____ (miss) my train. So I ⁴_____ (get) to the concert hall at nine o'clock, not eight o'clock.

A ⁵_____ you _____ (see) the show?

B Yes. The concert ⁶_____ (start) at 8:30, so of course, when I ⁷_____ (go) in, the band ⁸_____ (play). But I ⁹_____ (see) about 75% of the show. And it's the best concert I ¹⁰_____ ever _____ (see)!

Irregular past participles

4 **Write the past participles of the verbs.**

1 think _____   **6** go _____

2 ride _____   **7** see _____

3 have _____   **8** win _____

4 drink _____   **9** eat _____

5 read _____   **10** wear _____

5 Complete the sentences with the correct verbs from Exercise 4.

0 Someone has ___*drunk*___ my orange juice!

1 This book is great. I've _____ it five times.

2 We haven't _____ the movie yet. Is it good?

3 Zac loves motorcycles, but he's never _____ one.

4 I have a suit, but I've never _____ it.

5 Sara isn't here. She's _____ to the park.

6 My team's never _____ a game!

6 Complete the sentences with the correct forms of the verbs.

0 No ice cream, thanks. I've ___*eaten*___ (eat) enough.

1 Oh, you're from Peru? I _____ (think) you were Spanish.

2 This is an interesting article. Have you _____ (read) it?

3 Louis has _____ (lose) his keys. Do you have them?

4 We _____ (run), but we still missed the train.

5 They _____ (go) to bed late last night, so they're tired today.

6 I know I've _____ (see) that man before, but I can't remember where.

7 Zoe _____ (wear) her new dress to the party last week.

8 We _____ (ride) 30 km on our bikes yesterday.

Losing things

7 🔊 W.02 Put the conversation in order. Then listen and check.

☐ **Jack** What did you lose?

☐ **Jack** So what did you do? Did you find it?

☐ **Jack** What! That's not losing something – that's just a story about being messy!

1 **Jack** Have you ever lost anything really important?

☐ **Jack** How did you find it? Where was it?

☐ **Jack** That's terrible! How did you feel?

☐ **Darcy** My cell phone. It wasn't expensive, but it had all my stuff on it.

☐ **Darcy** Well, I got my mom's phone and I called my number. I heard it ringing. It was somewhere in my bedroom. I looked in the wardrobe. It wasn't there. Then I looked under the bed and there it was.

☐ **Darcy** It was the worst thing! It was like losing my whole life.

☐ **Darcy** Yes, I have.

☐ **Darcy** Yes, luckily I did.

8 Read the conversation again. Answer the questions.

0 What did Darcy lose?
   She lost her cell phone.

1 How did she feel about losing it?
   _____

2 Why did she feel this way?
   _____

3 How did she find it?
   _____

4 Where did she find it?
   _____

5 What does Jack think about her story?
   _____

Furniture

9 Put the letters in order to make items in a house.

0 keds ___*desk*___

1 elvsesh _____

2 pretac _____

3 reshwo _____

4 otilte _____

5 votse _____

6 foas _____

7 rirrmo _____

8 archmira _____

9 bedrarow _____

10 nustaric _____

11 palm _____

10 Which of the items in Exercise 9 might you find in each room? Some items might be in more than one room.

1 bedroom
   wardrobe

2 living room
   _____

3 kitchen
   _____

4 dining room
   _____

5 bathroom
   _____

SUMMING UP

11 Circle the correct words.

A Why didn't you come to the game yesterday?

B Oh, I was busy. I ⁰*painted* / *was painting* my bedroom. I still ¹*haven't finished* / *didn't finish*.

A Are you just changing the color of the walls?

B No, I have some new things, too. Last weekend, I ²*bought* / *have bought* a new desk and some ³*shelves* / *curtains* for the window. I want to get a new lamp, too. But I ⁴*didn't see* / *haven't seen* anything I like yet.

A There's a new store in town. I saw it when I ⁵*shopped* / *was shopping* last week. They have some nice lamps.

B Thanks. I'll go and have a look.

C EATING AND DRINKING
Buying and talking about food

1 Complete the questions with the words in the list.

> have any | everything | How many | else
> How much | Would you like | help you

0 Do you _____have any_____ of those Florida oranges?

1 Is that _____ ?

2 Can I _____ ?

3 _____ would you like?

4 _____ some of those?

5 Anything _____ ?

6 _____ is that?

2 🔊 **W.03** Complete the conversation with the phrases in Exercise 1. Then listen and check.

Assistant Good afternoon. ⁰_____Can I help you?_____

Customer Yes, I'd like some apples, please.

Assistant ¹_____

Customer Six big ones, please.

Assistant OK, ²_____

Customer Yes. ³_____

Assistant I'm afraid we don't have any. We have some really nice ones from California. ⁴_____

Customer Sure. I'll take three.

Assistant ⁵_____

Customer Yes, it is. ⁶_____

Assistant That's $5.20 altogether.

Customer Here you are.

Assistant And 80 cents change. Thanks!

3 Circle the correct words.

0 I think there are *some* / *any* eggs in the fridge.

1 We don't want *some* / *any* cake, thanks.

2 I'd like 500 grams of cheese and *some* / *any* chicken.

3 Sorry. There isn't *some* / *any* rice left.

4 You don't have *some* / *any* butter in your sandwich.

5 This soup is really good. Try *some* / *any*.

In a restaurant

4 Put the words in order to make sentences. Write W (waiter) or C (customer).

0 I / the / please / can / menu, / see
_____*Can I see the menu, please?*_____ [C]

1 ready / you / are / order / to
_____ ? [ ]

2 OK / everything / is
_____ ? [ ]

3 much / too / chicken / the / salt / on / there's
_____ . [ ]

4 can / please / have / check, / the / we
_____ ? [ ]

5 a / please / four, / for / table
_____ . [ ]

5 Complete the sentences with *much* or *many*.

0 There are too _____*many*_____ people in this restaurant.

1 There's too _____ salt in this soup.

2 There are too _____ things on the menu.

3 There's too _____ noise in here.

4 There are too _____ vegetables on my plate.

5 This restaurant's a little expensive. I can't spend too _____ money.

6 🔊 **W.04** Match the sentences in Exercise 5 with the replies. Then listen and check your answers to Exercises 5 and 6.

a You're right! It's disgusting. [ ]

b Eat them! They're good for you. [ ]

c Yes, I really don't know what to choose. [ ]

d Don't worry. It's your birthday, so I'll pay. [ ]

e Well, it's always busy at lunchtime. [0]

f Yes, let's go somewhere quieter. [ ]

Stores

7 Look at the pictures. Write the type of store.

1 _____

2 _____

3 _____

4 _____

Things you have to do

8 (Circle) the correct words. Then match the sentences with the pictures in Exercise 7.

a You *have to / don't have to* tell the barista what size drink you want. ☐

b You *have to / don't have to* wait here. ☐

c You *have to / don't have to* try clothes on over there. ☐

d You *have to / don't have to* keep medicines away from children. ☐

9 What do these customer notices mean? Write sentences with *have to* or *don't have to*.

0 "Buy now, pay later."

<u>You can have the item now, but you don't have to pay for it yet.</u>

1 "Please ask an assistant before trying on clothes."

_____

2 "Cash only – no credit or debit cards accepted."

_____

3 "We can deliver your groceries to your home."

_____

SUMMING UP

10 Complete the conversations. Write one word in each space.

0 A Why are you going to the _department store_ ?

B To buy a birthday present for Mom.

1 A My pen is broken.

B Well, you don't _____ to buy a new one. You can use mine.

2 A I'd like _____ olives, please. 250 grams.

B OK, here you are. Anything _____ ?

3 A What's the matter?

B I don't feel well. I ate too _____ cookies.

D LOOKING AHEAD
Plans and arrangements

1 Look at Abbi's schedule. Write her plans for the day.

SCHEDULE
TODAY
8 a.m. – go for a swim with Lola
10 a.m. – walk in park with Harry
1 p.m. – lunch with Mom and Dad
3 p.m. – dentist
6 p.m. – train to Chicago
9 p.m. – movie with Emily

0 At 8 a.m., ___*she's going for a swim with Lola.*___

1 After that, _____

2 At 1 p.m., _____

3 Two hours later, _____

4 At 6 p.m., _____

5 Finally, at 9 p.m. _____

2 Read the sentences and write I (intention) or A (arrangement).

0 We're having a coffee, too. [A]

1 They're going to travel there by bus. ☐

2 She's going to have yogurt and cereal. ☐

3 We're meeting at the new shopping mall. ☐

4 I'm just having a check-up – I hope. ☐

5 We're seeing Bradley Cooper's latest movie – I can't wait. ☐

3 Write about four arrangements you have for this week.

_____

_____

_____

_____

Sports and sport verbs

4 (Circle) the correct words.

0 Do you want to *go / do /* (play) volleyball later?

1 We *went / did / played* skiing last weekend.

2 My friend Alex *goes / does / plays* rock climbing every weekend.

3 You have to *go / do / play* gymnastics on Fridays.

4 I hate tennis. I never want to *go / do / play* it again!

5 Mom *goes / does / plays* running every morning.

6 We go to the sports center on Sundays to *go / do / play* some track and field.

7 Let's go to the gym. We can *go / do / play* karate.

Travel plans

5 **Match the parts of the sentences.**

0 We arrived late at the train station and missed ☐ *f*

1 It was late and we were tired, so we took ☐

2 My mom's car is at the garage, so I rode ☐

3 My friends left the movies at 10 p.m. and caught ☐

4 Last year we flew ☐

5 Dad really wanted to get home, so he drove ☐

a my bike to school today.

b the last bus home.

c to Colombia for our vacation.

d a taxi home from the airport.

e all night.

f the train by three minutes.

6 **Write five sentences about the transportation you use in your life.**

0 *When we go on vacation, we usually fly.*

1 _____

2 _____

3 _____

4 _____

5 _____

7 🔊 **W.05** **Listen to the conversation and answer the questions.**

0 Where is Martha going for her vacation?

She's going to California.

1 How long is she going for?

_____

2 How is she getting there?

_____

3 When is she leaving?

_____

4 What does she need to buy in town?

_____

5 Why is Ben surprised?

_____

8 🔊 **W.05** **Complete the conversation with the words in the list. Then listen again and check.**

> flying | going | going to be | going to buy
> ~~going to take~~ | going to spend | leaving
> taking | taxi | train

Ben Are you ⁰ *going to take* a vacation this year?

Martha Yes. We're ¹_____ two weeks in California.

Ben Lucky you. Are you ²_____ ?

Martha No, we're not. We're ³_____ the train. It's ⁴_____ a real adventure.

Ben That sounds really exciting.

Martha Yes, in fact, we're ⁵_____ next Monday. We're taking a ⁶_____ to the station and then it's the ⁷_____ all the way to Los Angeles.

Ben So, are you ready for the trip?

Martha Almost. I'm ⁸_____ to town tomorrow to buy a few last-minute things.

Ben Like what?

Martha Well, I'm ⁹_____ some more summer clothes and then I need to go to the pharmacy.

Ben The pharmacy? Why?

Martha I have to get some sunscreen.

Ben Sunscreen? But it's only May. It isn't hot enough to lie on the beach!

Martha Here it isn't, but it is in Los Angeles!

SUMMING UP

9 **Complete the email. Write one word in each space.**

Jack
Jackjones@thinkmail.com

Hi Jack,

You know our school volleyball team won the local championship last year, right? Well, this month we're playing teams from other cities in the US.

Next Saturday, we're ⁰ *playing* against a team in Colorado. It's a long way, so we aren't ¹_____ the train – we're ²_____ there! I've never been on a plane before, so I'm really excited.

We're going to stay in Colorado until Monday. On Sunday, I hope to ³_____ some rock climbing. There are some great places for it up there. My friend Sebastian wants to ⁴_____ skiing, but I don't think there's enough snow.

I'll write when we come back and tell you all about it.

Bye for now,

Alessia

1 INCREDIBLE PEOPLE

Grammar rap!

▶ 02

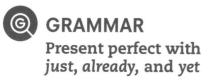 **GRAMMAR**

Present perfect with just, already, and yet

→ SB p.14

1 ★☆☆ Complete the sentences with *just, already,* or *yet.*

My little sister is really smart.

1 She's _____ learned to walk. She took her first steps last week.

2 She hasn't learned to read _____ , but she likes the pictures.

3 She's _____ learned to count from one to five and she's only one year old!

2 ★★☆ Look at Alex's to-do list for cleaning his bedroom. Write sentences with *already* and *yet.*

- clean desk ✓
- clean the floor ✗
- pick up towels and put them in bathroom ✗
- make bed ✓
- empty trash ✗
- hang up clothes ✓

Alex has *already cleaned his desk.*

_____

_____

_____

Alex hasn't _____

_____

_____

_____

3 ★★★ Look at the pictures. What has just happened? Write sentences with the verbs in A and the words in B, and *already, just,* or *yet.*

A	B
~~wake~~	~~up~~
fall	a goal
have	an accident
score	down
start	a trophy
win	to rain

0 *He has just woken up.*

1 They _____

2 They _____

3 She _____

4 She _____

5 It _____

Present perfect vs. simple past → SB p.17

4 ★☆☆ **Match the questions with the answers.**

0 Have you ever played volleyball? `b`
1 Where did you play? ☐
2 Did you enjoy it? ☐
3 Were you good at it? ☐
4 Has your team played against teams from other countries? ☐
5 Has your team won any trophies? ☐

a No, I wasn't.
b Yes, I have.
c Yes, we've already won three competitions.
d At school.
e No, we haven't – not yet.
f No, not very much.

5 ★★☆ **Complete the conversation. Use the present perfect or the simple past and the information in parentheses.**

It's Sunday afternoon.

Lucas Mom, I'm bored. What can I do?

Mom (finish your homework?)
⁰Have you finished your homework?

Lucas (last night)
Yes, I finished it all last night.

Mom (clean your room?)
1 _____

Lucas (yesterday)
2 _____

Mom (changed the water in the fish tank?)
3 _____

Lucas (before lunch)
4 _____

Mom (wash your bike?)
5 _____

Lucas (on Friday)
6 _____

Mom (call Jamie?)
7 _____

Lucas (this morning)
8 _____

Mom (watch that new movie on Netflix?)
9 _____

Lucas (last night)
10 _____

Mom Well, I don't know. What about coming to the supermarket with me?

Lucas Um … maybe not!

6 ★★★ **Complete the text. Use the present perfect or simple past form of the verbs in the list. You can use some verbs more than once.**

> be | buy | d̶o̶ | get | have | live | take
> not finish | not learn | stop | work

My grandmother is 65 and ⁰_____*has done*_____ a lot of things in her life. She 1_____ born in the country and 2_____ on a small farm until she was 16. She 3_____ in many different places, but she always says the farm 4_____ the best place of all. She 5_____ school because she started working when she was 15. She 6_____ many different jobs in her life – she 7_____ a children's nurse, a dressmaker, and a sales assistant, among other things. She 8_____ in a very expensive store in Chicago for several years. She 9_____ working after she 10_____ married. She 11_____ five children and she 12_____ care of the house. Grandma loves new things. She 13_____ just _____ a laptop, but she 14_____ how to use social media yet. I'm going to her house to help her now.

GET IT RIGHT!

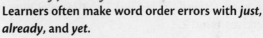

Present perfect with *just*, *already*, and *yet*

Learners often make word order errors with *just*, *already*, and *yet*.

✓ I **have just** finished my homework.
✗ I ~~just have~~ finished my homework.
✓ He has not **passed his exam yet**.
✗ He has not ~~passed yet his exam~~.
✓ We **have already finished** our project.
✗ We ~~already have finished~~ our project.

Correct the sentences.

0 I already have sent a message about the party to my friends.
I have already sent a message about the party to my friends.

1 My brother has yet not had a summer job.
_____

2 My big sister already has learned to drive.
_____

3 My family and I have been just on vacation.
_____

4 Have you yet bought your mom a birthday present?
_____

5 The singer has released already five albums.
_____

6 I just have uploaded some photos.
_____

 **VOCABULARY**
Personality adjectives

→ SB p.13

1 ★★☆ Circle the correct answers.

0 An active person	**A** loves theater.	**B** is always doing something.	**C** sleeps a lot.
1 A brave person	**A** takes risks when it's necessary.	**B** is often angry.	**C** doesn't like talking.
2 A creative person	**A** often makes mistakes.	**B** has original ideas.	**C** works very hard.
3 A charming person	**A** is very good-looking.	**B** has a lot of money.	**C** is kind and friendly.
4 A cheerful person	**A** often feels sad.	**B** enjoys life.	**C** often gets angry.
5 A laid-back person	**A** is very relaxed.	**B** can't wake up in the morning.	**C** never goes out.
6 A confident person	**A** doesn't work hard.	**B** believes in himself/herself.	**C** will keep a secret.
7 A positive person	**A** sees the good in everything.	**B** is frightened of the future.	**C** is often bored.
8 A talented person	**A** has a lot of money.	**B** isn't good at sports.	**C** is very good at something.

2 ★★☆ **Read the text. Complete the adjectives. The first and last letters are given.**

My ideal friend is very ⁰a_ctive_____ – that's important because I love sports and I want her to play basketball on my team. She's ¹c_____g and knows how to have fun, so she's a good person to hang out with. I need a friend who's really ²c_____e and is good at art, because I'm not and she could help me and give me some ideas.

Maybe it would be good if she was ³c_____l too – people sometimes say I'm too ⁴s_____s and don't laugh much. I'd like her to be ⁵p_____e as well – I don't like it when people only see the bad side of things.

3 ★★★ **Write one or two sentences about people you know (friends or family). Use the adjectives in Exercises 1 and 2.**

_____
_____
_____
_____

Collocations

→ SB p.17

4 ★★☆ **Complete the sentences with the correct form of the verbs in the list. Use each verb twice.**

| do | form | get | ~~have~~ | lose | make | take |

0 Jonah didn't ___have___ any homework last night.

1 The singer Leila Jenson _____ an appearance in this movie.

2 How many presents did you _____ for your birthday?

3 Hundreds of people have _____ their lives in the hurricane.

4 I need more information before I can _____ an opinion.

5 The children _____ a really good time at the zoo yesterday.

6 Rebecca wasn't on time for school all week. She's _____ a bad reputation for being late!

7 Hurry up! You _____ a music lesson in ten minutes.

8 Wait a minute. I want to _____ a photograph.

9 We _____ a group to collect money for the hospital.

10 That isn't right! You've _____ a mistake.

11 I know it isn't very good, but I _____ my best.

12 Oh, no! We've _____ the race. Our team is last.

13 Emily doesn't like _____ risks. She likes to be safe.

14 Have they _____ enough work for today?

WordWise: Phrases with just

→ SB p.15

5 ★★☆ **Check (✓) the five sentences that can be completed with *just*.**

0 I've ... cleaned the floor. ✓
1 That horror movie, *The Blob,* is ... terrifying. ☐
2 He can't tell you if you don't ... ask. ☐
3 This dress is almost ... perfect. ☐
4 The flower show was ... amazing. ☐
5 He's ... a child, but he's a talented artist. ☐
6 No problem, it was ... a thought. ☐
7 Gemma has ... called. She's on her way. ☐

6 ★★☆ **Match the five sentences in Exercise 5 with the meanings of *just*.**

1 a short time ago ☐0
2 only ☐
3 really ☐

REFERENCE

serious

cheerful

brave

positive

Personality adjectives

talented

creative

active

laid-back

charming

COLLOCATIONS

make a mistake / an appearance

do your best / work

get a present / a reputation

lose a race / your life / something important / your home

take a risk / a photo

form a group / an opinion

JUST

It was **just** a joke.

Tom's **just** arrived.

The book was **just** fantastic!

 # VOCABULARY *EXTRA*

1 Complete the sentences with the words in the list.

amusing | bossy | curious | reasonable | reliable | smart

0 Amy's _____amusing_____ . She makes me laugh.

1 Coral's _____ . She's intelligent and knows a lot.

2 Aidan's _____ . He's fair and makes good decisions.

3 Zara's _____ . She always tells us what to do.

4 Seth's _____ . He always does what he has promised to do.

5 Jake's _____ . He's interested in how things work.

2 Think of a person you know for each adjective in Exercise 1.

0 bossy

_____My big brother is bossy._____

1 amusing

_____

2 curious

_____

3 reasonable

_____

4 reliable

_____

5 smart

_____

ALL IN A DAY'S WORK

Who are your heroes? We aren't talking about superheroes like Superman or Wonder Woman; we want to hear your opinions about *real* people who make big differences to other people's lives while they do their jobs. So, tell us about the people you think are heroes because of the amazing things they do every day as part of their work.

1 _____

A Theo

Paramedics – the people who drive ambulances and help in medical emergencies – are my everyday heroes. The other day, my grandpa had a bad fall. I tried to help him, but I couldn't do it by myself, so I called an ambulance. It arrived almost immediately and the paramedics helped Grandpa right away. They were very professional and worked quickly, but they were also friendly and cheerful. By the time Grandpa was in the ambulance, he was relaxed and smiling again.
Every time paramedics go out, it's an emergency and often a serious situation. Think how many people that team has helped already and how many lives it's saved!

2 _____

B Caitlin

My neighbor, Anna, is a firefighter and she does an incredible – and dangerous – job. Firefighters don't just put out fires, they also help in all sorts of emergencies. Anna's rescued people from rivers, helped people stuck in the snow and she often has to go to traffic accidents. Firefighters have to be brave, smart, and good at working on a team. As well as saving lives, they teach people how to prevent accidents. She says every day at work is different: even on quiet days, they have to be ready for action. Firefighters often take risks in order to rescue people. I really admire them for that.

C Jodie

I live on the edge of a big city and until last year there was nothing for teenagers to do. Kids hung out on the streets and some of them got into trouble. Then Jonas, a youth worker, arrived and everything changed!
He's positive and easygoing, but he's also serious about his job. He wants to help us discover our talents – "Be curious!" he says. He's organized a lot of new activities for us, from songwriting to rock climbing! I can honestly say he's made an enormous difference to our lives. We have interesting things to do now and a cool place to go in our free time. Jonas is our hero!

3 _____

📖 READING

1 **Read the article. Write the names of the jobs under the photos.**

2 **Read the article again. Write A, B, or C next to the sentences.**

This everyday hero …

0 has a lot of variety in his/her job. `B`
1 works with young people. ☐
2 helps teenagers during their free time. ☐
3 is interested in people's health. ☐
4 often works in frightening and dangerous situations. ☐
5 tries to introduce teenagers to new ideas. ☐
6 helps to make people get better. ☐

3 **CRITICAL THINKING** **Read the questions and circle the best answers.**

1 What do the everyday heroes in A, B, and C have in common?
   A They all save lives.
   B They all help other people.
   C They all change people's lives.
   Because …

2 What are the personalities of the everyday heroes in A, B, and C like?
   A They're caring and reliable.
   B They're friendly and popular.
   C They're brave and talented.
   Because …

DEVELOPING } *Writing*

A description of a person I know well

1 **INPUT** **Read the text that Poppy wrote about her friend Liam. Match the pictures with three of the paragraphs.**

 **1** ☐

 **2** ☐

 THEATER **3** ☐

A I'm writing about my friend, Liam. I've known him for three years. We met when he moved to a house on my street.

B He's a little older than me, but I always feel like he's much older! I think that's because he's very confident. He isn't afraid to disagree with adults. For example, I've never said, "No, I don't agree," to an adult, but Liam has! I admire him for that.

C Another good point is that he's very honest. If he doesn't like something, he says so. He never says, "Oh yes, it's great," just to be the same as everyone else. In fact, this is why some people at school don't like him very much, I think.

D Does he have any bad characteristics? Yes! He's forgetful. Last week, he promised to come to my house and help me fix my bike. But he didn't come. I waited, then I called him. He's honest, so he said, "Oh, no! I forgot. I'll come right now." And he did. He arrived with a big smile, saying, "I always forget. Sorry." How could I be angry?

E I hope we're going to be friends for a long time.

2 **Read the text again. Match the paragraphs (A–E) with the topics.**

0 Not-so-good things about Liam ☐ D
1 The first good thing about Liam ☐
2 Final comment ☐
3 Introducing Liam and how they met ☐
4 Another good thing about Liam ☐

3 **ANALYZE** **Which adjectives describe Liam? Check (✓) three.**

1 polite ☐   **4** confident ☐
2 honest ☐   **5** forgetful ☐
3 intelligent ☐   **6** talented ☐

4 **Look at the three boxes you checked in Exercise 3. What examples does Poppy give to show that these adjectives describe Liam?**

1 _____
   _____
2 _____
   _____
3 _____
   _____

 WRITING TIP: describing a person

- Introduce the person. Give his/her name and say when and where you met.
- Explain why you like him/her. Use different adjectives to describe his/her personality (good and bad points!) and give examples.
- Finish with a comment about your friendship or your hopes for the future.

5 **PLAN** **You are going to write about a person you know well. Choose a friend or a family member and write a plan. Use the Writing tip to help you.**

Introducing the person

_____

Good and/or bad things about him/her

_____

_____

Final comment

_____

6 **PRODUCE** **Write your description in 150–200 words. Use your notes from Exercise 5.**

🎧 LISTENING

1 🔊 **1.01** Listen to the conversation. Circle the correct words.

1 They're discussing *last weekend* / *going to a movie* / *their parents.*

2 They both like *an actor* / *a movie* / *New York.*

2 🔊 **1.01** Listen again. Mark the sentences T (true) or F (false).

0 Megan thinks last weekend was exciting. ☐T☐

1 A movie premiere is the first time a new movie is shown. ☐

2 Megan wants to go to the premiere of Noah Centineo's new movie. ☐

3 Megan thinks her parents will be happy for her to go. ☐

4 Joe has an aunt and uncle who live in New York. ☐

5 Joe doesn't want to go to the movie with Megan. ☐

6 Joe doesn't like Noah Centineo. ☐

7 Joe and Megan are going to talk to Megan's parents. ☐

3 🔊 **1.01** Listen again. Complete the conversations. Use no more than three words.

1 Megan   Well, you know that Noah Centineo is my favorite actor?

   Joe   Yes, of course ⁰____I know____ that. So ¹_____ ?

2 Megan   Well, I'm going to the premiere!

   Joe   Oh, that's a ²_____ !

   Megan   Oh? Do you really think so?

   Joe   Yes, you ³_____ do it. You've always wanted to meet him.

3 Megan   Wow, that's great! Thank you. I'm just worried that my parents … ⁴_____ , they won't like the idea.

4 Joe   I know what you mean. But, hey, you know what? You have to ⁵_____ !

PRONUNCIATION
Sentence stress Go to page 118. 🎧

DIALOGUE

4 🔊 **1.03** Put the conversations in the correct order. Then listen and check.

Conversation 1

☐ **A** We can put a basketball game together between our street and Nelson Street.

☐1☐ **A** I have an idea for the weekend.

☐ **A** Let's speak to some people about it now.

☐ **B** I'll come with you. We can do it together.

☐ **B** A basketball game? That's a great idea!

☐ **B** Yeah? What is it?

Conversation 2

☐ **A** Thanks, but I'm not sure if we can do everything before Saturday.

☐1☐ **A** Mark, why don't we have a party?

☐ **A** I don't know. Can people come on Sunday?

☐ **A** Well, the next day's Monday – that's why. You know, homework to do, that sort of thing.

☐ **B** A party? Yes! I'll help you if you want. Let's have it this weekend.

☐ **B** OK, so forget Saturday. But you should definitely do it. It could be Sunday.

☐ **B** Oh, don't worry about homework, Stella. Come on! You have to make this happen!

☐ **B** Yes, I think they can. Why not?

PHRASES FOR FLUENCY ⟶ SB p.18

5 Put the words in order to make phrases.

0 what / know / You ? *You know what?*

1 sure / you / are / ? _____

2 it / let's / face _____

3 that / and / that's _____

4 so / don't / think / I _____

5 of / sort / thing / that _____

6 🔊 **1.04** Complete the conversations with the phrases in Exercise 5. Then listen and check.

0 **A** Hurry up. The movie starts at 8:30.

   B ___Are you sure?___ I heard it starts at 9:00.

1 **A** How did the tennis match go?

   B I lost. _____ , I'm awful at tennis!

2 **A** So what did you do over the weekend?

   B Not much – read, watched TV, _____ .

3 **A** Oh, Dad! Can I please watch *The Voice*?

   B No, you can't. I said no TV _____ .

4 **A** I know it's raining, but let's go for a walk.

   B _____ ? I'm staying right here!

5 **A** This song's awesome.

   B Well, _____ . It's terrible.

B1 Preliminary for Schools

🎧 **LISTENING**
Part 1: 3-option multiple choice

1 🔊 **1.05** **For each question, choose the correct answer.**

1 What's the weather like now?

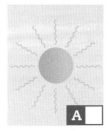 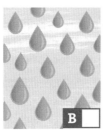 

5 Why is the girl excited?

  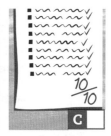

2 What are they going to have for dinner this evening?

  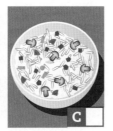

6 Where's the boy today?

  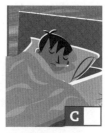

3 What job does the boy's aunt do?

7 How did the girl travel to her friend's house?

4 Where is the boy going to go first?

EXAM GUIDE: LISTENING PART 1

In B1 Preliminary for Schools Listening Part 1, you listen to seven short recordings. For each one, you have to answer a question by choosing one of three pictures.

• Read the questions carefully.
• Look at the three pictures and find similarities and differences between them.
• Identify the situation in each picture and think about the words you might hear.
• You will probably hear words from all the pictures, so don't choose a picture just because it contains the first word you recognise.
• Listen carefully to the dialogue and try to understand exactly what the speakers say about the things in the pictures.

2 A GOOD EDUCATION

▶ 05 Grammar rap!

© GRAMMAR
Present perfect with *for* and *since*

→ SB p.22

1 ⭐☆☆ **Complete the sentences with *for* or *since* and a number where necessary.**

0 Matthew has worked as a computer game tester ___*for*___ three years.

1 I've lived in this house _____ 2018.

2 We've only had our pet rabbit _____ six weeks.

3 Lauren has played the guitar in the band _____ she was 16 years old.

4 This tree has been here _____ more than 200 years!

5 I've written poems _____ I was ten years old.

6 Charlotte has been on the soccer team _____ 2019, so she has been a soccer player _____ _____ years.

7 Joshua has played tennis _____ he was four years old. He was born in 2012, so he has played tennis _____ _____ years.

2 ⭐⭐☆ **Write sentences. Use the positive or negative form of the present perfect and *for* or *since*.**

0 Thomas / not see / grandfather / two months
Thomas hasn't seen his grandfather for two months.

1 Shiloh and Joss / be / singers / five years
_____

2 Sophie / not play / tennis / she broke her leg
_____

3 Jacob / not write / his blog / a long time
_____

4 Dan / not go / to the dentist / a year
_____

5 You and I / be / friends / we were kids
_____

6 They / not see / a good movie / last summer
_____

7 We / not go / on vacation / two years
_____

3 ⭐⭐☆ **Jessie wants to ask her friends some questions for a school project. Complete them with the present perfect of the verbs.**

1 How long _____ (live) in your house?

2 What is your best friend's name? How long _____ (know) him/her?

3 How long _____ (be) at this school?

4 What's your favorite possession? How long _____ (have) it?

4 ⭐⭐⭐ **Look at the table and write answers to Jessie's questions. Use the present perfect and *for* or *since*.**

	Ella	Jack	Oliver
1	ten years	2010	three months
2	Sarah, 2018	Zayne, 2015	Dillon, a long time
3	five years	2019	September
4	bike, six months	dog, two years	laptop, May

1 Ella ___*has lived in her house for ten years.*___

2 _____

3 _____

4 _____

1 Jack _____

2 _____

3 _____

4 _____

1 Oliver _____

2 _____

3 _____

4 _____

5 ⭐⭐⭐ **Answer the questions in Exercise 3 for you.**

1 _____

2 _____

3 _____

4 _____

a, an, the, or no article   → SB p.25

6 ★☆☆ (Circle) the correct words.

Yesterday, I went to ⁰(*the*)/ *an* park. I go there a lot, so I know it very well. I sat on ¹*a* / *the* grass and started to read my book. Then, a lot of ²*the* / – things started to happen.

You can play ³*the* / – sports in the park, but ⁴*the* / – bikes aren't allowed. ⁵*A* / *The* boy on ⁶*a* / *the* bike was riding on the path. ⁷– / *A* police officer started to run after ⁸*a* / *the* boy, but she couldn't catch him.

There were three small children playing ⁹– / *the* soccer, too. One of them kicked ¹⁰*a* / *the* ball and it hit ¹¹*a* / *the* boy on his bike and he fell off. So the police officer caught him! I think this was ¹²– / *the* really bad luck for the boy.

7 ★★☆ Complete the text with *a, an, the,* or – (no article).

People have kept ⁰_–_ cats as pets for thousands of years. In ancient times, ¹_____ most important reason for keeping animals was for food or ²_____ work. Cats are ³_____ example of how ⁴_____ animals can help ⁵_____ people, because they catch ⁶_____ rats and ⁷_____mice.

These days, people keep cats as pets. Pet cats have ⁸_____ good life. They often sleep all day and people give them ⁹_____ tasty food they don't have to catch! Owners love their cats and think of them as members of ¹⁰_____ family.

8 ★★☆ Read the sentences. Check (✓) the four that are grammatically correct.

1 I love the birds. ☐
2 I saw a beautiful bird in the park yesterday. ☐
3 The bird in the park was bigger than mine. ☐
4 It was flying in a sky. ☐
5 I think the bird was a parrot. ☐
6 I think the birds make really good friends. ☐
7 There are many different sizes of the birds. ☐
8 I saw a picture of the biggest bird in the world. ☐

PRONUNCIATION
Word stress Go to page 118.

9 ★★★ Look at Exercise 8 again. Rewrite the four incorrect sentences so that they are correct.

_____
_____
_____
_____

GET IT *RIGHT!*

a(n) and no article
Learners often use *a(n)* where no article is needed, and no article where *a* is needed.

✓ I had *a* great time with my friends last Saturday.
✗ ~~I had great time with my friends last Saturday.~~

Complete the sentences with *a(n)* or – (no article).

0 I have ___*a*___ pet cat.
1 My brother works as _____ chef in a hotel.
2 Do you need to book _____ accommodations?
3 We haven't had _____ vacation since last year.
4 I'm _____ student at Columbia University.
5 We need _____ information about this right away.
6 I would like to buy _____ desk.

VOCABULARY
School subjects → SB p.22

1 ★☆☆ **Put the letters in order to make school subjects.**

0 You probably need a piano if you're a (scium) teacher. _____*music*_____

1 We often use computers in information (thecloongy). _____

2 (reggyhoap) teachers don't need maps now that there's Google Earth. _____

3 We have our (stichryme) classes in one of the science labs. _____

4 I love learning (shEling) because I want to visit London. _____

5 A calculator can be useful in a (tham) class. _____

6 I really enjoy (troyish) lessons when they're about people, not just dates. _____

7 Our (amard) teacher has been on TV and acted in a movie! _____

2 ★★☆ **Look at the photos. Write the subjects.**

0 _____*math*_____   **4** _____

1 _____   **5** _____

2 _____   **6** _____

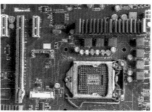

3 _____   **7** _____

Verbs about thinking → SB p.25

3 ★☆☆ **Find ten words about thinking.**

W	R	U	O	R	T	G	K	O	B	R
C	O	N	C	E	N	T	R	A	T	E
S	G	F	G	M	I	K	E	E	Y	B
G	T	E	U	E	E	B	A	S	E	T
I	H	G	E	M	I	H	L	I	H	I
M	I	N	S	B	E	L	I	E	V	E
A	N	S	S	E	L	V	Z	Y	K	E
G	K	G	L	R	T	E	E	N	Q	L
I	F	V	U	J	X	O	L	O	K	E
N	S	U	P	P	O	S	E	G	F	L
E	U	O	M	B	W	O	N	D	E	R
P	R	E	C	O	G	N	I	Z	E	C

4 ★★☆ **Complete the text with the words in Exercise 3.**

Do you ⁰b*elieve*_____ in the idea of morning people and night people? I do. I've always found it difficult to ¹c_____ in the morning. I can never ²r_____ anything when we have a test in the morning.

I ³w_____ why schools don't start in the evening. I ⁴t_____ night people would love that. Can you ⁵i_____ starting school at 8 p.m.? Great! We could sleep all day! But I ⁶s_____ morning people would hate studying at night.

You can always ⁷r_____ morning people – they're so cheerful in the mornings and don't seem to ⁸r_____ that night people don't want to chat! So, am I a morning person or a night person? You can ⁹g_____ , can't you?

5 ★★★ **Read and answer the questions so they are true for you.**

1 Do you believe everything you read in magazines?

_____

2 What kind of thing(s) do you remember easily?

_____

3 What time of day do you concentrate best?

_____

4 What do you imagine you will be in the future?

_____

REFERENCE

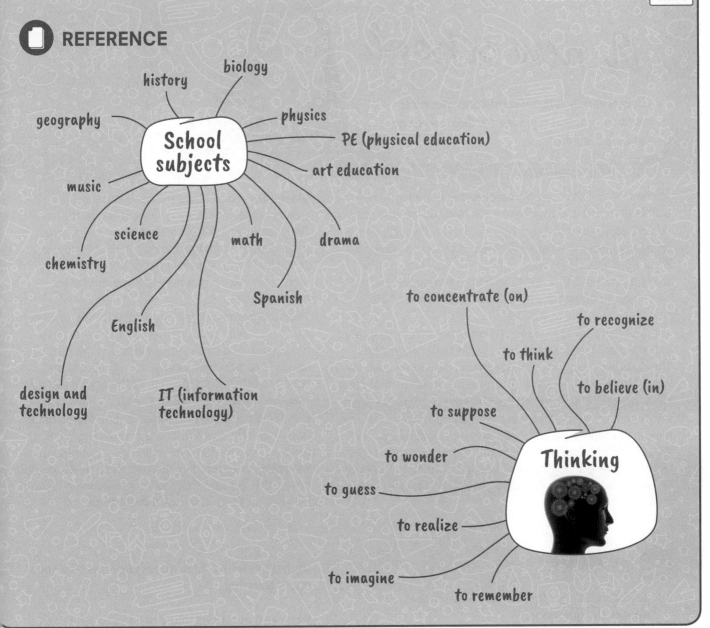

VOCABULARY *EXTRA*

1 Complete the definitions with the words in the list.

civics | economics | French | photography | robotics

0 In _____civics_____ class, you study the laws, politics, and economy of your country.

1 _____ is the study of how they make and use automated machines.

2 In _____ class, you learn to speak the language of France.

3 _____ is the study of money and business.

4 In _____ , you learn how to take good photos.

2 Write your school timetable in English. Write the days of the week, the times of the day and the subjects.

	Monday	Tuesday
9:00	Math	Chemistry
10:00	PE	Drama

A new school

Lucy's family left California and moved to New York when she was 13. She had to go to a new school …

I remember it really well. My parents drove me to my new school and said goodbye to me. I **[A]** walked into the school. I didn't know what to feel. I was excited and scared and a bit nervous, all **[B]**. There were a lot of other kids around. They were already in groups of friends, but none of them said hello or anything. It was a strange feeling for me, like I didn't really belong there. I wanted to be somewhere else, **[C]**.

The first thing I had to do was register, so I went to a room in the school that had a sign that said "Administration." They started asking me **[D]** questions. Suddenly, I felt like I was some kind of criminal. Then I went off to my first class. Wow, my first class was horrible. Perhaps it was because my accent or my clothes were different, but everyone just looked at me in such a strange way. And just like when I arrived, no one came to talk to me. Incredibly, that's still never happened: no one has ever taken the time to **[E]** or like me. I have friends because I made the first move to meet people.

Maybe the worst class that day, though, was science. The teacher wasn't too bad. She introduced me **[F]** and showed me where to sit. But the other students? Well, they looked at me like I was a guinea pig or something they were going to use for an experiment. I hated every minute.

Then there was a break and I went to sit somewhere alone, **[G]**. But I thought they'd want me to keep trying, so I tried to be more positive in the next class. That didn't go so well, though. Everyone talked to other students, **[H]**. At the end of the day, I couldn't wait to get out of there.

But since I first started at the school, things have gotten better. Now I'm doing fine and I get OK grades. I've learned a lot of things – but not what the teachers teach. I've learned that I'm strong and brave. I've learned that I will succeed even if some things aren't the way I want them to be.

📖 READING

1 Read about Lucy's first day at a new school. Answer the questions.

0 How did she feel about the school at the end of the first day?
She couldn't wait to leave.

1 What things made her feel bad?
_____

2 What surprised her most about the school?
_____

3 How does she feel about the school now?
_____

4 What has she learned from being at this school?
_____

2 Read the text again. Match the phrases with the correct places (A–H).

0 at the same time	B
1 but I sat by myself	☐
2 missing my mom and dad	☐
3 but that wasn't possible	☐
4 took a deep breath and	☐
5 to the class	☐
6 all kinds of	☐
7 get to know me	☐

3 <u>Underline</u> two or three things Lucy says that you find interesting.

4 Write two questions that you'd like to ask Lucy. Then write what you think she'd say in reply.

0 Q *What's your favorite subject at school?*
   A *Science. I like IT, too.*
1 Q _____
   A _____
2 Q _____
   A _____

5 CRITICAL THINKING Read the questions and circle the best answers. Then explain why.

1 Which sentence best describes Lucy's feelings now?
   A I always feel sorry for new students.
   B I'm enjoying the classes and doing very well.
   C It was hard, but my experience was useful.
   Because …

2 What do you think was the worst thing for Lucy?
   A the unfriendly students
   B being in a different part of the country
   C the new school system
   Because …

An informal email

1 **INPUT** **Read the email quickly. Check (✓) the things Ryan talks about.**

   1 how he feels about his routine ☐

   2 the things he likes to watch on TV ☐

   3 homework that he doesn't like to do ☐

   4 a party for his birthday ☐

2 **Read the email again and answer the questions.**

   1 How does Ryan feel about weekdays?

   _____

   2 What has changed in Ava's life?

   _____

   3 Why can't Ryan write a longer email?

   _____

3 **ANALYZE** **Find the short forms of the phrases below in the email. Complete them with the words in the list.**

   | I | Is | I̶t̶ ̶w̶a̶s̶ | I have |

   0 _____It was_____ good to get your last email.

   1 _____ everything going well?

   2 _____ hope you can come.

   3 _____ a lot to do.

4 **Read the email again. Find phrases that express these things.**

   0 What Ryan says instead of *How are you?*:
      ___*How's it going?*___

   1 Two ways that Ryan starts to talk about a different topic: _____ and
      _____

   2 Direct questions Ryan asks Ava:
      _____ and _____

   3 Three ways he checks that Ava understands what he's saying: _____ ,
      _____ , and _____

   4 How he ends his email: _____

Ava
Avasmith@thinkmail.com

Hi Ava,

How's it going? Good to get your last email – it was fun to read. I liked hearing about your life, your routine, and stuff, so I thought I could tell you about mine.

Most weeks are the same, but I guess that's true for everyone, right? Monday to Friday, well, they're school days, so that's a kind of routine. You know, get up at 7:30, go to school at 8:45, come home at 4:00 and do homework, then have dinner, and go to bed. Of course, a lot of things make every day different, so I don't mind the routine. It's cool. We don't have the same classes at school every day and I do different things in the evenings.

Anyway, I wonder how you're doing at your new school. Everything going well? I'm sure it is!

By the way, it's my birthday next month – I'll be 15!! We're having a party on Saturday 12th.

Hope you can come. Let me know, OK?

So, what was I saying about routine and things? Yeah, right, homework – got a lot to do, so I'm going to stop here. I really, really want to hear from you again soon, OK?

Take care,

Ryan

 WRITING TIP: an informal email

- Start your email by saying hello: *Hi, Hey, ...* .
- First, ask how your friend is.
- Then say what you're writing about and why.
- Finish with a friendly expression.
- Use informal language. Imagine you are talking to your friend and use:
  - short sentences and contracted forms
  - direct questions
  - a friendly/informal style.

5 **PLAN** **You are going to write an email to an English-speaking friend. Your friend wants to know about your weekend routine. Write a plan using the Writing tip to help you.**

   _____

   _____

   _____

   _____

6 **PRODUCE** **Write your email using informal language in 150–200 words. Use your plan from Exercise 5.**

🎧 LISTENING

1 🔊 **2.03** **Listen to the three conversations. Match them with the correct photos. There is one photo you don't need.**

A ☐

B ☐

C ☐

D ☐

2 🔊 **2.03** **Listen again. Circle the correct answers.**

1 What is Kate asking to do?
  A go home because she feels sick
  B have extra time to finish some work
  C miss the biology class on Friday

2 Why won't Lily lend Max her skateboard?
  A She's going to use it later.
  B She's doesn't trust Max to take care of it.
  C She doesn't know where it is.

3 What does the boy want to do?
  A stay out later than usual
  B have a party at home
  C invite Freddie to stay

DIALOGUE

3 🔊 **2.04** **Put the conversations in the correct order. Then listen and check.**

1 | 1 | Girl | Excuse me. Is it OK if I try this shirt on?
  ☐ Girl Really? OK. Can I try a size 8, too?
  ☐ Girl OK, thanks.
  ☐ Girl I think so. This is a size 10.
  ☐ Woman Well, I think it might be too big for you.
  ☐ Woman Of course you can. Here's a size 8. OK. Tell me when you're finished.
  ☐ Woman Of course. Do you have the right size?

2 | 1 | Milo | Will, can I ask you something?
  ☐ Milo Great, thanks. Oh – another thing.
  ☐ Milo Well, I forgot to charge my cell phone. Can I take yours?
  ☐ Milo I understand. Thanks anyway.
  ☐ Milo Can I borrow your jeans tonight – you know, the white ones?
  ☐ Will Sure. What is it?
  ☐ Will Sorry, no way! My phone goes with me everywhere.
  ☐ Will Yeah, go ahead. I'm not wearing them.
  ☐ Will Another thing? What is it?

Train to TH!NK

Thinking about texts

4 **Read the text about Lucy on page 22 again. Circle the correct answers.**

1 Where *wouldn't* you find this text?
  A in a magazine
  B on a website
  C in a newspaper
  D in a homework book

2 What is the main purpose of the text?
  A to complain about bad schools
  B to describe a personal experience
  C to entertain the reader
  D to persuade readers not to change schools

3 What is the best title for the text?
  A What I learned in a school that I didn't like
  B My first day at school
  C Good and bad teachers
  D How to do well at a new school

B1 Preliminary for Schools

 READING
Part 4: Gapped text

1 Five sentences have been removed from the text below. For each question, choose the correct answer. There are three extra sentences which you do not need to use.

The Global  Teacher Prize

There are plenty of prizes for good students but now there is an award for the best teacher in the world. ¹_____ It aims to celebrate the work of teachers and recognise how important their work is. The organisers believe that good teachers can change the lives of their students for the better.

The award started in 2015. It is open to all teachers in every country of the world. In its first year, over 5,000 teachers from 127 countries took part. So far, the winners have come from the US, Palestine, Canada, the UK and Kenya. ²_____ Every year the winner receives one million dollars to spend on education in their community.

The 2019 winner was a teacher called Peter Tabichi. He teaches in a village school in a semi-desert area of Kenya. His class, like all the classes in his school, has over 50 students in it. Most of his students are from very poor families and the school has hardly got any classroom furniture and very little equipment. ³_____ Despite these problems, this teacher started a 'talent club' to help his students. Some of them have even taken part in international science competitions. He also gives extra help to students with difficulties and regularly meets their families. ⁴_____ In only three years, Tabichi's class has grown from 200 to 400 students.

⁵_____ In fact, the chosen teachers are always very proud of their success. However, they know they are only there because of their students. For a small school in a poor area, the prize money can make a huge difference to the school, its present and future students, as well as the whole local community.

A It only has one computer and a very slow internet connection.

B Tabichi was very excited to be chosen as the winner.

C The headteacher of the school was very proud.

D This new prize is called the Global Teacher Prize.

E Ten students from the school went to university last year.

F As a result, more teenagers have started going to the school.

G The students only enjoy some of the lessons at the school.

H The subjects they teach are varied too, and include Maths, English and Art.

EXAM GUIDE: READING: PART 4

In B1 Preliminary for Schools Reading Part 4, you read a text with five gaps. You have to choose the missing five sentences from eight options.

• Read the text quickly for general understanding.
• Look at the sentences. Remember there are three extra sentences.
• Read the sentences before and after each gap.
• Choose a sentence from A–H and try it in the gap.
• Re-read to check if the new sentence makes sense with the information surrounding the gap.
• Re-read the text with all the completed gaps to make sure the whole text makes sense.

CONSOLIDATION

🎧 LISTENING

1 🔊 2.05 Listen and (circle) the correct option: A, B, or C.

  1 When did Freya start at the school?
    A Wednesday
    B Friday
    C Thursday
  2 What is Freya's favorite subject?
    A science
    B art
    C Spanish
  3 Where does Aaron offer to take Freya?
    A the library
    B the cafeteria
    C the gym

2 🔊 2.05 Listen again and answer the questions.

  0 How many days has Freya been at the school?
    four days
  1 How does it compare to her old school?
    _____
  2 Who is her favorite teacher? What does he teach?
    _____
  3 Why is Freya good at Spanish?
    _____
  4 Where is the library?
    _____

Ⓖ GRAMMAR

3 **Correct the sentences.**

  0 I've been at Lincoln High School since two years.
    I've been at Lincoln High School for two years.
  1 It's a biggest school in our city.
    _____
  2 I've yet taken some important exams.
    _____
  3 But I haven't gotten the results already.
    _____
  4 I've yet decided what I want to study in college.
    _____
  5 I want to study the Spanish.
    _____
  6 Bella is the my best friend at school.
    _____

🅰z VOCABULARY

4 **Match the sentences.**

  0 He's so brave. [d]
  1 Your sister's so laid-back. [ ]
  2 Have you heard Jim play the trumpet? [ ]
  3 My grandma's so active. [ ]
  4 Ethan's the most positive person I know. [ ]
  5 Ms. Harrington's really cheerful. [ ]

  a Yes. He's so talented!
  b She's always doing something.
  c He can see the good in absolutely everything.
  d He isn't scared of anything.
  e She always has a big smile on her face.
  f Does she ever get angry?

5 **Write the subjects these students are studying.**

0 Oh, no! I have paint all over my shirt.
art

1 I love acting in front of the rest of my class. It's so much fun.
_____

2 The capital of Italy is … is … Oh, what is it?
_____

3 Twelve percent of 200 is 24, isn't it?
_____

4 I like learning about the past, but why do we have to learn all those dates?
_____

5 I can't believe it. I've forgotten my tennis racket.
_____

6 I love doing these experiments. They're so much fun.
_____

7 We're practicing a song for the end-of-year concert.
_____

DIALOGUE

6 🔊 **2.06** **Complete the conversation with the phrases in the list. Then listen and check.**

> Are you sure? | I'll help you if you want.
> I've decided | just | Let's face it
> Of course you can. | That's a great idea.
> that sort of thing. | You know what?

Ben ⁰*I've decided*_____ to start a homework club.

Chloe A what?

Ben A homework club. It's so we can get together, discuss our classes, help each other with our homework, ¹_____

Chloe ²_____ Can I be in it?

Ben ³_____ I want you to be in it!

Chloe ⁴_____ I could text some people.

Ben OK. Who are you thinking of?

Chloe What about David?

Ben David? ⁵_____ He's way too smart. He doesn't need our help. ⁶_____ , he won't want to join.

Chloe Yes, but he doesn't have many friends. Maybe he'd like to join to make friends.

Ben ⁷_____ You might ⁸_____ be right.

Chloe I might.

Ben In fact, it's perfect. We help him make friends and he helps us with our homework. Chloe, you're a genius!

📖 READING

7 **Read the text. Mark the sentences T (true) or F (false).**

0 Mrs. Millington started teaching 15 years ago. ☐ F

1 Although she's a good teacher, she needs a bit more experience. ☐

2 Students are well behaved in her classes. ☐

3 She really loves the subject she teaches. ☐

4 She worked for a travel company before she became a teacher. ☐

5 She has worked in different countries around the world. ☐

6 One reason she changed jobs is because she wanted to work near home. ☐

7 Although she's a great teacher, she's sometimes a bit unfriendly. ☐

My Science teacher, Mrs. Millington, is a really amazing person.

She's in her forties, but she's only been a teacher for five years. You'd never know she doesn't have very much experience, because she's excellent in the classroom. She never has any trouble from students because her classes are so fascinating that everyone just listens to everything she says. She's really enthusiastic about science and knows how to make her class interesting.

Before she was a teacher, she spent more than 20 years working as a research scientist. She worked at a lab in Australia for two years. She also took part in some international experiments, so she's traveled a lot. She brings all these experiences into the classroom and she explains why science is so important in the real world. She loved her job, but she got tired of traveling so much and she wanted to work regular hours. That's when she made the decision to become a teacher. It seemed to be the perfect opportunity to finally follow her dream. I'm so happy she did. She's such a warm and positive person that when you're in her classes, you don't even feel you're at school.

✏️ WRITING

8 **Research a person who is famous for doing charity work. Write a paragraph (about 150–200 words) about him or her. Include the following information:**

- who the person is
- what charity work he/she does
- what makes him/her so special

Grammar rap!

▶ 08

 GRAMMAR

Comparative and superlative adjectives (review) → SB p.32

1 ★☆☆ **Complete the table.**

Adjective	Comparative	Superlative
big	bigger	0 _the biggest_
1 _____	taller	2 _____
3 _____	4 _____	the prettiest
expensive	5 _____	6 _____
7 _____	more interesting	8 _____
9 _____	10 _____	the most difficult
good	11 _____	12 _____
13 _____	worse	14 _____

2 ★★★ **Complete the text with the correct form of the adjectives.**

I've just seen *First Man* and I can say that it's
0 _____the most amazing_____ (amazing) movie I've
ever seen. It's excellent. The special effects are
incredible. They're ¹_____
(realistic) than any other special effects I've seen.
You feel like you're in space with the actors. I really
like space movies. I thought *Gravity* was really exciting,
but *First Man* is even ²_____
(exciting). Ryan Gosling and Claire Foy are two of
³_____ (professional) actors
in Hollywood and they do some of the
⁴_____ (good) work of
their careers in this movie. Of course, the fact
that Ryan Gosling is ⁵_____
(handsome) man in the world helps! The movie
is playing at the Odeon until Friday. Tickets are
⁶_____ (cheap) in the
afternoon than in the evening and the movie theater
is ⁷_____ (empty) then, too.
But whatever you do, don't miss it!

PRONUNCIATION
Words ending with -er /ər/
Go to page 118. 🎧

(not) as … as comparatives → SB p.32

3 ★☆☆ **Look at the information about two movie theaters. Mark the sentences T (true) or F (false).**

Adjective	The Roxy	The Gate
price	$12	$10
number of seats	230	170
friendly staff	*	***
age of building	1920	2010
distance from your house	1.2 km	0.7 km
overall experience	***	***

0 The Roxy is more expensive than the Gate. — T
1 The Roxy is smaller than the Gate. — ☐
2 The Gate isn't as friendly as the Roxy. — ☐
3 The Gate is older than the Roxy. — ☐
4 The Roxy isn't as close as the Gate. — ☐
5 The Roxy isn't as good as the Gate. — ☐

4 ★★☆ **Complete the sentences about the movie theaters with the correct form of be, (not) as … as and the adjectives.**

0 The Roxy _isn't as cheap as_ (cheap) the Gate.
1 The Roxy _____ (friendly) the Gate.
2 The Gate _____ (big) the Roxy.
3 The Roxy _____ (modern) the Gate.
4 The Gate _____ (far) the Roxy.
5 The Gate _____ (good) the Roxy.

5 ★★★ **Complete the second sentence so that it means the same as the first. Use no more than three words.**

0 There has never been a movie series as good as *Star Wars*.
Star Wars is the _____the best_____ movie series ever.

1 The movie is disappointing compared to the book.
The movie isn't _____ the book.

2 *Avengers: Endgame* is the most successful movie of all time.
No movie has been _____ *Avengers: Endgame*.

3 *Toy Story 4* is funnier than *Toy Story 3*.
Toy Story 3 _____ as *Toy Story 4*.

4 *Spider-Man* and *Superman* are equally bad.
Spider-Man is _____ *Superman*.

Making a comparison stronger or weaker

→ SB p.33

6 ★★☆ Look at the pictures. Mark the sentences ✗ (not true), ✓ (true), or ✓✓ (the best description).

0

Owen — Callum

A Callum is taller than his brother. `✓`
B Callum is a lot taller than his brother. `✓✓`
C Callum isn't as tall as his brother. `✗`

1

Floyd 143   140 Ramsey

A Floyd is heavier than Ramsey. ☐
B Floyd isn't as heavy as Ramsey. ☐
C Floyd is a bit heavier than Ramsey. ☐

2

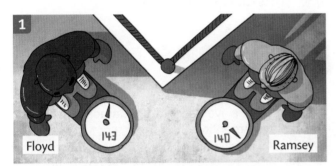

A $15   B $150

A B isn't as expensive as A. ☐
B B is much more expensive than A. ☐
C A is cheaper than B. ☐

3

Ellie 99%   Ruby 25%

A Ruby's test was far worse than Ellie's. ☐
B Ellie's test was better than Ruby's. ☐
C Ellie's test wasn't as good as Ruby's. ☐

7 ★★★ Complete the sentences so that they are true for you. Use *a lot, much, far, a little,* and *a bit*.

0 I ___am much shorter than___ my best friend.
1 Math _____ English.
2 Playing sports _____ playing video games.
3 Chocolate _____ apples.
4 Winter _____ summer.
5 Rabbits _____ goldfish.

Adverbs and comparative adverbs

→ SB p.34

8 ★☆☆ Mark the underlined words ADJ (adjective) or ADV (adverb).

0 He plays soccer <u>worse</u> than I do. ___ADV___
1 Her German is <u>better</u> than mine. _____
2 He speaks <u>more clearly</u> than you. _____
3 You walk <u>more quickly</u> than me. _____
4 It's raining a lot <u>harder</u> today. _____

9 ★★☆ Complete the sentences with the correct form of the words in parentheses.

"Why can't you be more like your cousin Kyle?" my mom always says.

0 He talks to adults ___more politely___ (polite) than you.
1 He studies _____ (hard) and always does _____ (good) than you at school.
2 His bedroom is _____ (clean) than yours.
3 He runs _____ (quick) than you.
4 He writes _____ (careful) than you.
5 He treats me _____ (kind) than you.

GET IT RIGHT!

Comparatives and superlatives

Learners often incorrectly use *better* instead of *best* and *last* instead of *latest*.

✓ Friday is the **best** day of the week.
✗ Friday is the ~~better~~ day of the week.
✓ I use the internet to get the **latest** news.
✗ I use the internet to get the ~~last~~ news.

Circle the correct words.

0 This theater always shows the *last* / (*latest*) movies.
1 I don't think pizzas are *best* / *better* than hamburgers.
2 Was it the *last* / *latest* one left in the store?
3 It was one of the *best* / *better* days of my life!
4 He likes to wear the *last* / *latest* fashion.
5 It's the *best* / *better* restaurant I know.

VOCABULARY
Movie genres

→ SB p.32

1 ★★☆ **Read the clues and complete the crossword. Who is the mystery movie character?**

This type of movie …

0 is often set in the future or in space.

1 is always exciting, with a lot of car chases, explosions, and special effects.

2 makes you laugh.

3 is exciting and a little scary at times, too.

4 is always scary.

5 tells you about the real world.

6 is popular with children.

7 involves a love story and some laughs.

```
 0
 S  C  I  F  I
       1
    2
 3
       4
    5
    6
    7
```

2 ★★☆ **Read the quotations. Write the movie genre you think they come from.**

0 "Quick! We have 60 seconds to stop the bomb from exploding!" ___action movie___

1 "Deep in the caves of Colombia lives a bird that few people have ever seen." _____

2 "The next Mars shuttle leaves at 3 p.m. Meet me at the space station." _____

3 "Come on, Barney Bear. We have a problem to solve." _____

4 "I love you, Brad. I've always loved you. You're just too proud to know it!" _____

5 "Did you see its face? I tell you – that thing isn't human!" _____

6 "It was a rainy Thursday evening in New York – the perfect time for a murder." _____

7 "Why would I want to be a member of a club that would have me as a member?" _____

Types of TV shows

→ SB p.35

3 ★★☆ **Put the letters in order to make types of TV shows.**

0 kalt hows ___talk show___

1 swen _____

2 elyairt ohws _____

3 madra _____

4 nocrato _____

5 mage wohs _____

6 cimtos _____

7 opsa proae _____

8 roptss whos _____

9 latent whos _____

4 ★★★ **Write the types of TV shows.**

WHAT'S ON?

0 "Tonight there's live action from Maracana where Brazil plays Argentina." ___sports show___

1 "Who will win the final of *The It Factor*: Jasmine and her amazing dog Scooby or the boy band Zap?" _____

2 "On the sofa tonight, answering Paula Nightingale's questions, is actor Lewis James." _____

3 "Tonight on *Win It Or Lose It*, three couples compete for the top prize of $50,000." _____

4 "Catch up on today's stories from the US and around the world. Followed by the weather." _____

5 "Minnie has a chance to make things right between Josie and James, but will she take it?" _____

WordWise: Expressions with *get*

→ SB p.33

5 ★☆☆ **Complete the sentences.**

0 The show doesn't finish until 11 p.m., so I don't think we'll get h___ome___ before midnight.

1 I don't know how to get t_____ , so I need to look at the map.

2 Lee got very a_____ about the soccer game. They lost again.

3 You look really thirsty. I'll get you a d_____ .

4 After resting and taking his medicine for a week, he got b_____ .

5 It's an exciting movie. You won't get b_____ .

REFERENCE

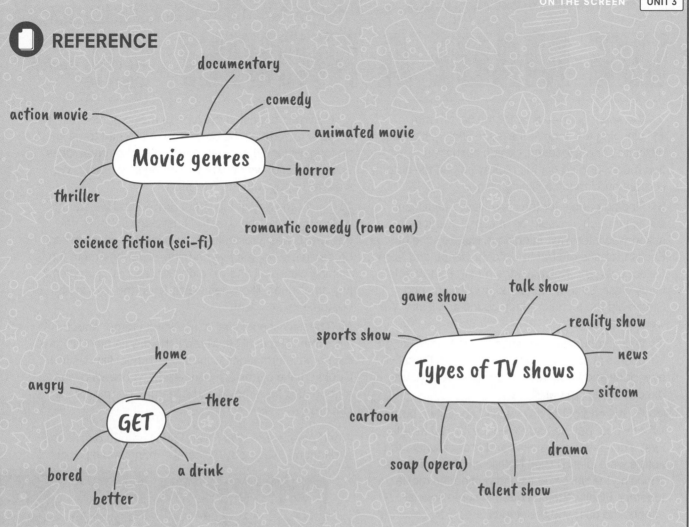

documentary

comedy

action movie

Movie genres

animated movie

horror

thriller

romantic comedy (rom com)

science fiction (sci-fi)

home

angry

GET

there

bored

a drink

better

talk show

game show

reality show

sports show

Types of TV shows

news

sitcom

cartoon

drama

soap (opera)

talent show

VOCABULARY *EXTRA*

1   Write the words in the correct column.

adventure | cooking | superhero | travel | ~~western~~

Movie genres		Types of TV shows	
_____western_____	movie	_____	show
_____	movie	_____	show
_____	movie		

2   Write the name of a movie or TV show as an example of each one.

0   western   _The Magnificent Seven_

1   travel   _____

2   superhero   _____

3   cooking   _____

4   adventure   _____

3   Which movie genres and TV shows do you like? Write your top three lists for each.

Favorite movie genres

1 _____

2 _____

3 _____

Favorite types of TV shows

1 _____

2 _____

3 _____

WE MADE A MOVIE!

By Olivia Garton, Class 4B

A We spent our free time for the next month planning the shoot – that's the filming. It's really difficult to find a location, design costumes, find music, and so on. Mr. McKay helped the actors prepare and I made a filming plan.

B Finding people for the crew wasn't as difficult as I thought it would be because everyone I asked was interested in doing it. Natalie's the best at English, so she offered to write the script, and Aaron, Caleb, Lola, and Katya are the most talented actors in my class, so they signed up, too. Penny and Stefan did the technical stuff: sound and lights. We were ready to go!

C It all started last year when I took a filmmaking course at summer camp. It's the best thing I've ever done and I decided I'm going to be a movie director when I'm older!

D By the end of the day we had about two hours of video, but we had to reduce it to 20 minutes. First, I deleted the mistakes and scenes where the actors were joking. Then Natalie and I spent hours choosing the best scenes and putting the movie together. Finally, Stefan added in some special effects, the title, and the credits.

E However, choosing the type of movie genre wasn't as easy as forming the crew! The movie had to be short, no longer than 20 minutes. We had a lot of great ideas and in the end, we decided on an original drama. We were all happy with the final story.

F Finally, the day of the shoot arrived and we started filming. I was the director! I used the school's new camera. It was stressful! I don't think I've ever worked harder in my life, but I've certainly never had more fun. Filming went well and we didn't have any big problems – just small ones, like when Caleb fell in the river in his costume by accident!

G The new school year started and I forgot about filmmaking until Mr. McKay, the drama teacher, gave me some information about a high school film festival. Could I make a movie, I wondered? All I needed was a good idea for a movie and a team of people for the film crew.

World premiere of *Wild River*! Friday at 4:30 p.m. in the auditorium. Everybody welcome – bring some popcorn!

READING

1 **Read the article. Put the paragraphs in order.**

1 _C_   3 ___   5 ___   7 ___
2 ___   4 ___   6 ___

2 **Read the article again. Mark the sentences T (true) or F (false). Correct the false information.**

0 Olivia wants to be a script writer when she is older. ☐ F
   She wants to be a movie director.

1 One of Olivia's teachers asked her to make a movie. ☐
_____

2 Olivia couldn't find the right people for the movie. ☐
_____

3 It was more difficult to choose the movie genre than to form the film crew. ☐
_____

4 There was a lot of preparation to do before filming. ☐
_____

5 The day of filming was the busiest day in Olivia's life. ☐
_____

6 They deleted the most exciting scenes from the movie. ☐
_____

3 **CRITICAL THINKING** **Read the questions and ⟨circle⟩ the best answers. Then explain why.**

1 Did Olivia and her classmates work together well?
   A no
   B yes
   C We can't know the answer to this.
   Because …

2 Olivia wrote this article to
   A describe a new experience.
   B encourage students to make movies.
   C explain how to make a movie.
   Because …

A for and against essay

1 **INPUT** Read the essay quickly. Does the writer agree with the title?

_____

2 Read the essay again. Do you agree with the writer? Think of one additional argument to support *your* opinion.

_____

_____

3 **ANALYZE** Complete the sentences with the letters A–D.

1 Paragraph _____ agrees with the essay title.
2 Paragraph _____ disagrees with the essay title.
3 Paragraph _____ gives the writer's opinion.
4 Paragraph _____ is a general introduction to the topic.

4 The <u>underlined</u> words in the essay are linking words. Put these linking words in groups of the same meaning.

> however | in addition | in conclusion
> in my opinion | moreover | on the other hand
> personally | to sum up | what's more

Finally	Also
1	1
2	2
	3

But	I think
1	1
2	2

"Going to the movies is a waste of time." Discuss.

A Everyone loves going to the movies. <u>However</u>, we can watch movies at home on TV, online, or on DVD. So, is going to the movies a waste of time?

B A visit to the theater can be expensive. Tickets aren't cheap and snacks cost a lot. Streaming a movie or buying a DVD is cheaper and you can watch it as many times as you like. Watching a movie on a widescreen television with digital audio, is nearly as good as being in a movie theater. <u>Moreover</u>, what's more fun than inviting your friends, making popcorn, and having a movie night at home?

C <u>On the other hand</u>, a trip to the movies is an enjoyable way to spend time with friends. <u>What's more</u>, modern theaters offer you an amazing experience: comfortable seats, huge screens, and excellent sound systems. You get so involved in the movie that you feel like you're part of it!

D <u>To sum up</u>, I think going to the movies is a good way to spend time. For me, it's definitely the best way to enjoy a movie. <u>Personally</u>, I don't go to the movies very often, so when I do, it's really special.

 WRITING TIP:
a for and against essay

- Organize your essay into paragraphs:
  1 Introduce the topic in general
  2 Agree with the title
  3 Disagree with the title
  4 Conclusion with your opinion
- Use linking words to connect your ideas.
- Use formal language.

5 **PLAN** You are going to write a for and against essay with the title: "Watching television is a waste of time." Think of some ideas for and against the title, then write a plan. Use the Writing tip to help you.

6 **PRODUCE** Write your essay in about 200 words. Use your plan from Exercise 5.

🎧 LISTENING

1 🔊 **3.03** Listen to the four conversations. Match them with the correct photos.

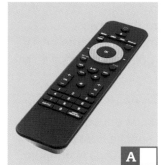 **A** ☐

 **C** ☐

 **B** ☐

 **D** ☐

2 🔊 **3.03** Listen again and answer the questions.

0 Why does the man change his mind about getting some help?

Because he drops the TV and wants help to clear it up.

1 Why can't the man open the web page?

_____

2 What DVD does the sales assistant recommend?

_____

3 Why won't the TV work?

_____

DIALOGUE

3 🔊 **3.04** Put the words in order to make requests and offers. Then listen and check.

Offers

0 any / help / you / do / need
Do you need any help? _____ ?

1 help / I / you / can
_____ ?

2 OK / everything / is
_____ ?

Requests

3 something / you / help / could / with / me
_____ ?

4 hand / lend / you / me / can / a
_____ ?

5 few / you / minutes / do / have / a
_____ ?

4 Match the offers and requests in Exercise 3 with the replies. Sometimes there is more than one correct answer.

a No, I'm all right. ☐

b Sure – what is it? ☐

c I do, actually. ☐ 0

d Not really. I can't get the TV to work. ☐

e Of course I can. ☐

f Sure. Now, let me see. ☐

5 Write a short conversation about the picture.

PHRASES FOR FLUENCY → SB p.36

6 🔊 **3.05** Put the conversation in the correct order. Then listen and check.

☐ **Phoebe** I always knew I would be. In fact, I had a dream about it when I was a little girl.

☐ **Phoebe** Well, this one did!

1 **Phoebe** Guess what? I got a part in a soap opera!

☐ **Phoebe** I am. Have a look. It's a letter from the TV company.

☐ **Oscar** What? You're kidding!

☐ **Oscar** Oh, come on! Dreams don't mean anything.

☐ **Oscar** Wow! It's true! Looks like you're going to be famous after all.

7 🔊 **3.06** Complete the conversations with the phrases in the list. Then listen and check.

> after all | come on | ~~Guess what~~ | have a look
> In fact | Looks like

Conversation 1

A ⁰ *Guess what* ? I won the singing competition.

B Oh, ¹_____ ! You aren't a good singer.
²_____ , you're terrible!

A You're just jealous.

Conversation 2

A So did you fail the test?

B No, I got 95%!

A What?!

B Here – ³_____ if you don't believe me.

A It's true!

B ⁴_____ I'm pretty smart
⁵_____ !

B1 Preliminary for Schools

🎧 LISTENING
Part 2: 3-option multiple choice

1 🔊 3.07 **For each question, choose the correct answer.**

1 You will hear two friends talking about a film. What did the girl think of the film?

A It was really good.

B She enjoyed parts of it.

C She disliked the music.

2 You will hear a girl talking about an experience. What was it?

A a concert

B a song contest

C a talent show

3 You will hear two friends talking about a TV programme. What type of programme was it?

A a soap opera

B a reality show

C a sports programme

4 You will hear a boy talking about a book. How did he feel about it?

A amazed

B bored

C scared

5 You will hear part of a radio programme. What type of programme is it?

A a chat show

B the news

C a sports report

6 You will hear two friends making plans. What do they decide to do?

A go to the cinema

B go to a restaurant

C watch films at home

EXAM GUIDE: LISTENING PART 2

In B1 Preliminary for Schools Listening Part 2, you listen to six dialogues and answer questions by choosing one answer from three options. The questions are generally about opinions and attitudes, or a general question about the situation, not details or facts.

- Before you listen, read the questions and look at the options. This will give you a general idea about what you're going to hear.
- The first time you listen, choose an answer or eliminate an option you are sure is wrong.
- The second time you listen, make a final choice.

4 ONLINE LIFE

Grammar rap!

▶ 11

Ⓖ GRAMMAR
Indefinite pronouns (everyone, no one, someone, etc.)

→ SB p.40

1 ★☆☆ Circle the correct words.

The new

XR4

has landed!

It's ⁰(everything) / something you could want in a tablet and more.

It's so simple that ¹no one / anyone can use it, but if there's ²everything / anything you don't understand, our technical team is ready to help you.

Its amazing network coverage means you have internet access ³everywhere / somewhere you go.

If there's ⁴something / nothing you need to remember or somewhere you need to be, the alarm system will make sure you don't forget.

If you order before Christmas, there's ⁵nothing / everything to pay until March.

The new XR4 – ⁶someone / no one should leave home without it!

2 ★★☆ Complete the sentences with the words in the list.

> anyone | anything | anywhere | everyone
> no one | nowhere | something | somewhere

0 This party's boring. I don't know ___anyone___ .

1 I'm sure I've seen that man _____ before, but I can't remember when.

2 Ava's really enjoying her new school. _____ has been so friendly to her.

3 There are no seat numbers in this theater – you can sit _____ you like.

4 It wasn't me. I didn't do _____ , I promise!

5 Have you spoken to Connor? There's _____ he wants to tell you.

6 There are no trees here, so there's _____ to hide from the sun.

7 It's a secret. Tell _____ !

3 ★★★ Complete the second sentence so that it means the same as the first. Use no more than three words.

0 Leah is really popular. ___Everyone___ likes Leah.

1 I'm really bored. There's _____ do.

2 Are you hungry? Do you want _____ eat?

3 There's danger everywhere. _____ safe.

4 The cat has disappeared. I can't find _____ .

5 He's following me. He's _____ I go.

all / some / none / any of them

→ SB p.41

4 ★☆☆ Match the parts of the sentences.

0 We have hundreds of DVDs, but ___[c]___

1 I have a lot of pens, but ___[ ]___

2 There were ten teams in the competition, but ___[ ]___

3 Twenty students took the final test and ___[ ]___

4 The cats have already eaten, so ___[ ]___

a all of them passed.

b don't give any of them more food.

c we don't watch any of them now.

d none of them played very well.

e I don't think any of them work.

5 ★★☆ Complete the sentences with all, some, any, or none.

0 I have a lot of friends, but ___none___ of them remembered my birthday.

1 We like most of his movies, but _____ of them are awful.

2 They can't say which game they like best. They love _____ of them.

3 I don't like _____ of these songs. They're all terrible!

4 He has 2,000 stamps. _____ of them are very rare.

5 Three buses came, but _____ of them were full.

PRONUNCIATION
The short /ʌ/ vowel sound
Go to page 119. 🎧

should(n't), had better, ought to   → SB p.43

6 ★☆☆ **Match the sentences with the pictures.**

0 You should buy it. It looks good on you.   C

1 We ought to leave now. It's going to rain.   ☐

2 You'd better see a doctor about that.   ☐

3 There's a lot to do. We ought to start now.   ☐

4 You shouldn't touch those. They might be hot.   ☐

5 We'd better hide – quick!   ☐

7 ★★☆ **Write advice with the phrases in the list.**

> activate flight mode on your tablet │ attach it as a file
> ~~change to a different provider~~ │ choose a different password
> delete it │ go online and find it cheaper │ open it
> upload it onto your blog

0 My phone never has a signal.
You'd better change to a different provider.

1 I don't know who this email is from and it has a strange-looking attachment.
_____

2 This email has a lot of important information in it.
_____

3 I like this backpack, but it's $50. That's expensive!
_____

4 The plane's about to take off.
_____

5 This photo's really embarrassing. I don't want anyone to see it.
_____

6 I need to send this photo to Nico.
_____

7 This web page contains a lot of my personal information.
_____

GET IT RIGHT!

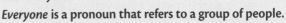

all vs. everyone

Learners sometimes confuse *all* and *everyone*.

***Everyone* is a pronoun that refers to a group of people.**

✓ At the theater, we bought popcorn for **everyone**.

✗ At the movie, we bought popcorn for ~~all~~.

***All* is used to modify a noun or pronoun.**

✓ My siblings **all** have cell phones.

✗ My siblings ~~everyone~~ have cell phones.

Complete the sentences with *everyone* or *all*.

0 I hope _____ *everyone* _____ likes the cake I've made.

1 My friends _____ have jobs.

2 There should be enough lemonade for us _____ to have some.

3 Has _____ finished their work?

4 Does _____ that you know have a laptop?

5 I would like to introduce myself to _____ members personally.

6 After that, _____ of us got a ball and tried to throw it as far as possible.

VOCABULARY
IT terms
→ SB p.40

1 ★★☆ **Match the parts of the sentences.**

0 Before take-off, please activate   `d`
1 Don't open that   ☐
2 I don't have any network   ☐
3 Our vacation is almost over and I haven't uploaded   ☐
4 If you can't buy it in the stores, go   ☐
5 To open that file, you need to install   ☐

a any photos to Instagram yet.
b coverage, so I can't make a call.
c this program first.
d flight mode on your mobile devices.
e attachment. It could have a virus.
f online and buy it.

2 ★★☆ **Complete the sentences with an appropriate verb.**

8 STEPS TO _____ ONLINE SECURITY

(0) Never _____*open*_____ an attachment if you don't know where it's come from.
(1) Think twice before you _____ a message on social media.
(2) Don't _____ photos of people onto social media sites without asking them.
(3) Be careful if you _____ in passwords in a public place.
(4) Always _____ emails that you don't want other people to read.
(5) Don't _____ apps from online stores you've never heard of.
(6) Don't _____ any files from websites you don't know.
(7) Check what a program is before you _____ it onto your laptop.

3 ★★★ **Complete the sentences.**

1 That's a great photo. You should u*pload*_____ it to your s_____ m_____ pages.
2 If you like making music, you should b_____ this a_____ . It helps you mix different songs.
3 I forgot to a_____ the f_____ before I sent the email.
4 I deleted the m_____ without reading it.
5 You need to enter your email address and then t_____ in your p_____ .
6 It takes a long time to d_____ big files.

Language for giving advice
→ SB p.43

4 ★☆☆ **Complete the sentences with advise or advice.**

0 Don't take his ___*advice*___ . He doesn't know what he's talking about.
1 Our teachers always _____ us not to leave our homework until the last minute.
2 I strongly _____ you not to call her after 8 p.m.
3 My mom always gives me good _____ .

5 ★☆☆ (Circle) **the correct answers.**

The most useful advice I ever got was from my grandfather. He said, "Never take ⁰ _*advice*_ from anyone." But I was only 18 and didn't know how useful it was, so I ¹_____ his advice and let people give me advice ²_____ everything. I ³_____ advice on what to wear and what to eat. My bank manager advised ⁴_____ save my money; friends advised me to spend it. My mother advised me to marry young; my father advised me ⁵_____ it. I got so much advice ⁶_____ so many people that I didn't know which advice to ⁷_____ and which advice to ignore. My grandfather was right. Now I've stopped ⁸_____ advice and life is much simpler!

0 (A) advice   B advise   C advisable
1 A took   B followed   C ignored
2 A about   B in   C over
3 A had got   B got   C had
4 A to me   B me to   C me for
5 A for   B against   C on
6 A from   B for   C with
7 A get   B offer   C follow
8 A taking   B giving   C ignoring

6 ★★☆ **Answer the questions for you.**

1 What are you good at giving advice about?
_____
_____

2 What's the worst advice you've ever had?
_____
_____

3 Whose advice do you always follow and why?
_____
_____

4 Are you good at taking advice? Why / Why not?
_____
_____

5 Do you like giving advice? Why / Why not?
_____
_____

7 ★★★ **Write about the best advice you've ever had (about 50 words). Who gave it to you and why was it good advice?**

REFERENCE

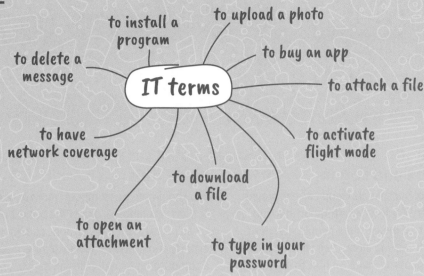

to install a program

to upload a photo

to delete a message

to buy an app

IT terms

to attach a file

to have network coverage

to activate flight mode

to download a file

to open an attachment

to type in your password

LANGUAGE FOR GIVING ADVICE

bad / good / practical / useful advice	to ignore (someone's) advice
advice about (something)	advisable
to ask for / get advice from (someone)	to advise (someone) (to do something)
to give / offer (somebody) advice	to advise against (something)
to take / follow (someone's) advice	

VOCABULARY *EXTRA*

1 Match the words.

0 click on	c		**a** tag
1 hash			**b** browser
2 like			**c** a link
3 web			**d** a file
4 video			**e** a photo
5 save			**f** call

2 Complete the sentences with the words in the list.

file | hashtag | liked | link | video call | web browser

0 Lois saved the _____*file*_____ and shut down the laptop.

1 My grandma lives really far away, but we _____ her every week so she can see our faces!

2 Which _____ do you use for research?

3 So, you open the page ... right, then click on the _____ and a new window opens.

4 That was a nice photo! I _____ it and shared it with all my friends.

5 Send your comments to # (_____) special days.

DIGITAL EXPERTS NEEDED!

Parents and grandparents always know who to ask when they have problems with their phones or digital gadgets – the nearest teenager, of course! So various organizations around the country have had the great idea of connecting teenage digital experts to people in need of help with technology. What's happening in your area?

Comments

(3) replies

A Phoebe and Logan

We're members of our school's Good Citizens project. So we spend every Wednesday afternoon at a club for senior citizens – that means older people who don't work anymore. They bring along their laptops, tablets, and phones to ask us for advice on how to use them. It's a simple idea and works really well! Most of their questions are about Skype and downloading photos and videos. These are great ways for people to keep in touch with family and friends living far away. I think what we do is a sort of exchange: they learn some digital skills from us and we learn more about life from talking to them!

B Noemi

I'm in the SOS Tech group at my youth club. There are about ten of us and we go to the community center every Saturday morning to teach people how to use their digital gadgets. All sorts of people come for help – it's not only older people that don't feel confident about using computers. The other day, I showed a woman how to do her shopping online because she couldn't drive after an operation on her leg. Another man came in with a new tablet. He decided he'd better learn to use it because he didn't want to be left behind! What do I get out of it? Well, I've discovered that I enjoy explaining things to people, so I'm thinking about becoming a teacher!

C Louis

You should see the computer room in our public library on a Tuesday evening! It's one of the busiest places in town. People can come in and ask for advice about technology. I'm on the team of experts and we try to help everyone. If you don't have access to a computer these days, life can be difficult. We help people find information online, show them how to fill out online forms, how to use job sites, things like that. At first, people are often embarrassed because they feel like they should know how to do these things. After we've explained what to do, they look relaxed and we're happy to share our skills. They think we're so smart, but I always tell them everything's easy when you know how to do it!

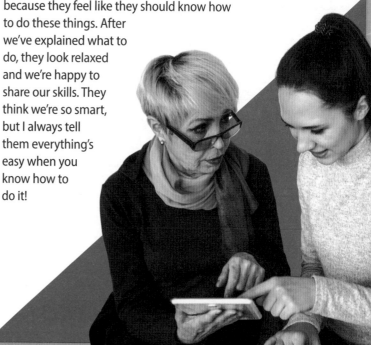

📖 READING

1 **Read the posts. Check (✓) the best title.**

   A Sharing your digital skills ☐

   B The trouble with technology ☐

   C Teens teach IT at school ☐

2 **Read the texts again. Write A, B, or C to answer the questions.**

   Which student …

   0 discovered something they enjoy? B

   1 helps people who sometimes feel embarrassed? ☐

   2 gives advice to elderly people? ☐

   3 helps people keep in contact online? ☐

   4 works on the weekend? ☐

   5 thinks technology is easy to deal with once you know how? ☐

3 **CRITICAL THINKING Who would say these things about the projects in the text? Mark each sentence A (the students) or B (the people they help).**

   B 0 I want to be able to use new technology.

   ☐ 1 It's so interesting talking to them.

   ☐ 2 It was a complete mystery, but now I understand.

   ☐ 3 They're very patient and explain things very clearly.

   ☐ 4 It's so easy for me and I feel I'm helping others.

   ☐ 5 You hear a lot of negative things about us, so it's good to show we aren't all bad!

DEVELOPING ⟩ *Writing*

A blog: giving advice

1 **INPUT** Read the blog entry quickly. Why is Johnny's father angry?

| Blog | About | News | Advice | Community | 🔍 |

TIPPS FOR EVERYDAY LIFE

Hi – I'm Johnny Tipp.
Welcome to my top "tipps" blog!

TIPP 1 — *What to do when your laptop stops working*

I'm writing on my ^{0} ___*tablet*___ because my laptop isn't working. A few days ago, I was writing my ^{1} _____ when a message appeared on the screen. It said there was a problem with my ^{2} _____ and I should restart it. So I did exactly that, but the same message reappeared. After repeating this five times, I realized the problem was serious, so I looked ^{3} _____ for a solution, using my phone. I found a site that promised to fix everything. But was it too good to be true? Here's what I learned …

TIPP 1.1 — *You should never trust sites that promise to "fix everything."*
I only had to ^{4} _____ a file onto my laptop and then ^{5} _____ it.

TIPP 1.2 — *You should never download files from sites you don't know.*
Next, a message appeared: "Please enter your credit card information." So, I used my dad's credit card.

TIPP 1.3 — *Never pay before you see results.*
Then the laptop ^{6} _____ everything on it, shut down, and hasn't worked since. When Dad got home, he was really tired from work, but I had to tell him the whole story.

TIPP 1.4 — *You shouldn't tell bad news to a tired person.*
He got very upset with me, and it didn't get any better when he found out that $1,000 was missing from his bank account!

2 Complete the blog entry with the words in the list.

> blog | deleted | download | install
> machine | online | ~~tablet~~

3 **ANALYZE** Read the blog entry again. Put the events in the correct order.

- [1] Johnny writes his blog.
- [ ] He tells his dad about the problem.
- [ ] He installs a program.
- [ ] His laptop tells him it has a problem.
- [ ] His laptop crashes.
- [ ] He goes online to find a solution.
- [ ] He uses his dad's credit card.
- [ ] He downloads a program.

WRITING TIP: giving advice

- Organize the advice into short steps. Use bullet points or numbers.
- The advice or instructions should be clear and easy to understand.
- Give examples from your own experiences.
- Use the imperative and *should / ought to / 'd better*.
- Write in a friendly style and use informal language.

4 **PLAN** You are going to write a blog entry giving advice.

1 Choose a topic you know something about or explain how to do something. For example: keeping a pet / making a cake / fixing a bike.
2 Make a list of the advice you want to include.
3 Organize the advice in order and write a plan. Use the Writing tip to help you.

5 **PRODUCE** Write a blog entry giving advice to your readers in 170–200 words. Use your plan from Exercise 4.

 **LISTENING**

1 🔊 4.02 Listen to William and Selena talking about passwords. According to Selena, which of these is a strong password?

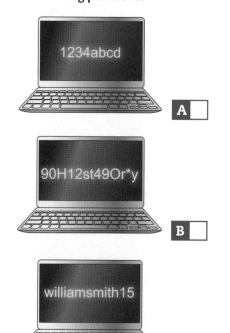

1234abcd

A ☐

90H12st49Or*y

B ☐

williamsmith15

C ☐

2 🔊 4.02 Listen again. Complete the sentences in William's notes with one or two words.

0 You should use a ___different___ password for every website.

1 You shouldn't _____ your passwords to other people.

2 A good password has numbers, _____ letters, lowercase letters, and punctuation marks.

3 If you use words that have a _____ _____ for you, they will be easier to remember.

4 It's best to never _____ _____ your password anywhere, so people can't find it.

5 Use numbers such as your lucky number, your house number, or your _____ _____ .

DIALOGUE

3 Put the words in order to make sentences.

0 shouldn't / password / use / always / you / same / everything / the / for
   You shouldn't always use the same password for everything.

1 other / you / password / tell / people / shouldn't / your

   _____

2 ought / password / good / a / letters and / have / in / numbers / it / to

   _____

3 difficult / guess / a / for / password / somebody / to / be / must / else

   _____

   _____

Train to TH!NK

Logical sequencing

4 Put the actions in a logical order.

1 ☐ Ask for some advice.
  ☐ Get some bad advice.
  ☐ Take the advice.
  ☐ 1 Have a problem.
  ☐ Get some good advice.
  ☐ Ignore the advice.
  ☐ Ask someone else.

2 ☐ Send your message.
  ☐ Write a reply.
  ☐ Add an attachment.
  ☐ Delete the first message.
  ☐ Log onto your email.
  ☐ Type in your password.
  ☐ 1 Go online.
  ☐ Read a message.

5 Connect the first and last events in the lists with your own ideas.

1 1 Find an old friend on a social networking site.
  2 *Send the friend a message asking about their life.*
  3 _____
  4 _____
  5 Delete the friend!

2 1 See a great new band on TV.
  2 _____
  3 _____
  4 _____
  5 Go and see their show.

B1 Preliminary for Schools

READING
Part 2: Matching

EXAM GUIDE: READING PART 2

In B1 Preliminary for Schools Reading Part 2, **you have to match the texts to the people.**

- Read profiles 1–5 and underline the important information.
- When you've read all the texts, go back and check that the text you've chosen matches the information in the profile <u>exactly</u>. If it doesn't, re-read the other options.

1 For each question, choose the correct answer.

The young people on the right all need to find some information online for a geography project.

Underneath, there are eight websites. Decide which website would be most suitable for each person.

1
Simon's geography project is about comparing cities around the world. He wants to see interviews with people talking about where they live and ways cities are protecting the environment.

2
Tara wants to research places that have difficult weather conditions. She'd also like to see how the population and industry of these locations is changing.

3
Marek needs to see the geography of each continent. He's keen to see the types of products regions are famous for and who they sell them to.

4
Aysha would like to research famous tourist attractions and see how many people visit them each year. She'd like to find historical photos of these attractions.

5
Pedro needs information about how countries move goods around to different locations. He also wants to know about festivals around the world and their history.

WEBSITES ABOUT WORLD GEOGRAPHY

A StudyCentre.cxm | StudyCentre.com lets you explore celebrations that cultures around the world have each year. Look at ways they've changed over time and see how ancient celebrations sometimes share similar traditions. Find details about the things different regions produce and the transport used to send them abroad or within their own homelands.

B history101.cxm | This website has some videos from the 1880s showing typical city street scenes. You can compare them with modern videos to see how cities around the world have grown and developed. Find details about the kinds of goods each region is well known for, and how this has changed over the past hundred years.

C info-point.cxm | Find out the kinds of things countries are most well known for making and which countries buy them from abroad. This data is updated annually, so you can see new trends with these goods. You are also able to access detailed maps that show a country's mountain ranges, rivers and lakes, and historic routes that were used for trade purposes.

D land-mark.cxm | Every country has landmarks that tourists from around the world come and visit. At land-mark.com, you can see pictures of these attractions and read the history behind them. There are also details of each country's most well-known celebrations and when they take place in cities all over the world.

E GreenData.cxm | Go to GreenData.com to compare which countries are world leaders at protecting their wildlife and forests. See pictures of national parks in each continent and the annual number of visitors. This website also shows the amount of rainfall each country has annually and the weather conditions in each region.

F Xplain.cxm | Xplain.com follows regional trends on every continent, so you can find how many people move to various locations because of work and business opportunities. It also shows how villages, towns and cities deal with anything from floods to incredible amounts of snowfall and what it's like to live in some of the hottest and coldest places on Earth.

G A2Z.cxm | This website is a great place not only to find facts about a country but also to see some of the oldest pictures available of important landmarks from all over the world. See how they have changed over time by looking at recent videos of them. A2Z.com also shows you the number of people who travel to them each year.

H Edu-Hub.cxm | This educational website provides the most recent data on each country's capital, so you can see their similarities and differences. Find out how each of these locations are reducing pollution and increasing green spaces in their downtown areas. Edu-Hub.com also has videos of teens sharing their stories about what it's like to grow up in these places.

CONSOLIDATION

🎧 LISTENING

1 🔊 **4.03** **Listen to the conversation. Check (✓) A, B, or C.**

1 What kind of show is *Priceless*?
- **A** a talk show ☐
- **B** a sports show ☐
- **C** a game show ☐

2 What time does *Let Him Go* start?
- **A** 8 p.m. ☐
- **B** 9 p.m. ☐
- **C** 11 p.m. ☐

3 What kind of movie is *Let Him Go*?
- **A** a sci-fi movie ☐
- **B** a horror movie ☐
- **C** a comedy ☐

2 🔊 **4.03** **Listen again and answer the questions.**

0 Why does Mike want to stay in?
Because he's a little tired.

1 What day of the week is it?
_____

2 What kind of movie is *By Tomorrow*?
_____

3 What happens in *Let Him Go*?
_____

4 What does Milly want Mike to make?
_____

🔤 VOCABULARY

3 **Look at the word snake. Find 12 types of movies and TV shows and write them in the correct column. Some can go in both.**

TV shows	Movie genres
	sci-fi

4 **Complete the text with the words in the list. There are three words you don't need.**

> against | attach | ~~buy~~ | download
> followed | for | ignored | type
> on | open | post | useful

One of the problems with modern technology is the number of passwords you need to remember. Every time I want to ⁰_____*buy*_____ an app, check my email, or ¹_____ a photo on social media, I have to ²_____ in a password. My laptop even sometimes asks for one if I want to ³_____ a file or ⁴_____ an attachment. What makes it worse is that all these passwords have to be different. So I asked a friend of mine ⁵_____ some advice. He advised me ⁶_____ keeping them on my laptop. He told me to write them all down in a file and send it to myself and keep it in my email inbox. It sounded like ⁷_____ advice, so I ⁸_____ it and did exactly what he said. So my passwords are all safely stored in my email inbox. The only problem is that I can't remember the password to access it!

🔍 GRAMMAR

5 **Rewrite the sentences with the words in parentheses.**

0 I don't know anyone kinder than her. (kindest)
She's the kindest person I know.

1 The movie was hated by everyone. (no one)
_____

2 You should study more if you have a test tomorrow. (better)
_____

3 The weather was a lot nicer yesterday. (worse)
_____

4 Jen is nearly as tall as Josh. (a bit)
_____

5 The best thing for you to do is to tell the truth. (ought)
_____

6 Is this house empty? (anyone)
_____

7 I'm a bad singer, but I'm better than Perry. (badly)
_____

8 It's really important for me to finish this today. (must)
_____

UNITS 3 & 4

DIALOGUE

6 🔊 **4.04** **Complete the conversation with the phrases in the list. Then listen and check.**

> after all | Can you lend me a hand?
> have a look | ~~do you have a few minutes?~~
> I can do it for you | In fact
> Is everything OK? | looks like | ought to

Vicky Ted, ⁰ _do you have a few minutes?_

Ted Sure. Yes, I do.
¹ _____

Vicky Not really. I'm trying to download this file, but it isn't working.
² _____

Ted Of course. Let me take a look.

[after a few minutes]

Ted That's very strange.
It ³ _____
you have a virus on your laptop.

Vicky A virus!

Ted Yes, ⁴ _____ .
Every time I try to open this window, it just shuts down.

Vicky Oh, no. Is it serious?

Ted Not really.
⁵ _____ ,
I had the same one on my laptop, so I know exactly what to do.

Vicky Great. So, can you fix it?

Ted Yes, I can. I'm just running a program now. But you really
⁶ _____
update your virus protection.
⁷ _____ ,
if you want.

Vicky Thanks. That would be great.

Ted Oh. Oh, no.

Vicky What?

Ted Well, it didn't do that before. It seems your laptop's completely dead. Very strange. Maybe I didn't know that virus ⁸ _____ .

📖 READING

7 **Read the text and match the phrases with the correct places (A–F). There is one phrase you don't need.**

0 you didn't have a chance of seeing it again   A

1 in the house

2 apart from things like live sports events,

3 like they did when my parents were children

4 whenever and wherever they like

5 better sound and

6 they watched the night before

BYE-BYE TV?

Hey everyone! While I was watching my favorite Netflix series on my tablet, I thought, does anybody still sit down and watch TV these days?

When my parents were growing up, people only had a few channels to choose from. If you missed your favorite show, it was just bad luck – **[A]** (unless you had a video recorder), but the TV was the focal point of the house. Families planned the shows they wanted to watch and made sure they finished their dinner before the show started. At school, children talked about the shows **[B]** and because there weren't many shows for kids, they all watched the same thing. Can you imagine that? Now there are tons of options!

When I was growing up, TV screens were bigger and a lot thinner than the TVs of my parents' time. We had **[C]** a remote control to change channels. But the TV was still an important piece of furniture **[D]** and we all sat around it on a Saturday night to watch something as a family.

Nowadays the TV just doesn't seem to be so important, and **[E]** people can choose what they want to watch and when they want to watch it. They don't even need to watch it on a TV. They can download or stream shows and watch them on their tablets and phones **[F]**, thanks to mobile devices. Watching TV has become a much more individual activity and in many houses the TV set sits forgotten in the corner of the room. Is it time to say goodbye to the TV?

✏️ WRITING

8 **Write a short text (about 120–150 words) about your favorite TV show. Include the following information:**

- what it is
- when you watch it
- what it's about
- why you like it

45

5 MUSIC TO MY EARS

▶ 14 Grammar rap!

GRAMMAR
Present perfect continuous
→ SB p.50

1 ★☆☆ **Match the sentences with the pictures.** <u>Underline</u> **examples of the present perfect continuous.**

0 They<u>'ve been watching</u> TV all evening. `A`

1 He's been waiting for a long time. ☐

2 It's been snowing for days. ☐

3 She's been running for 62 hours. She's trying to break the world record. ☐

4 He's been talking to them for hours. ☐

5 She's been playing her favorite instrument all morning. ☐

2 ★★☆ **Complete the sentences. Use the present perfect continuous (positive or negative) of the verbs.**

0 She's *been reading* (read) that book for more than a week now.

1 Dylan's in bed. He _____ (feel) well for about three hours.

2 Dinner's going to be good. Dad _____ (cook) all afternoon.

3 What awful weather. It _____ (rain) all day.

4 Lara looks really tired. She _____ (sleep) very well.

5 I _____ (study), so I don't think I'm going to pass this test.

3 ★★☆ **Complete the text. Use the present perfect continuous of the verbs in the list.**

> dream | talk | think | t̶r̶y̶ | write

I ⁰*'ve been trying* to contact you. Is your phone broken? I want to ask you a question: will you join "The Cool Four"? Jared, Nina, Zoë, and I have started a band! As you know, I ¹_____ songs for years, and I ²_____ of having my own band. I'm sure people ³_____ that I'd never do it. Well, they're wrong! Jared, Nina, and Zoë are here now, and we ⁴_____ about the name of the band if you join us! How does "The Cool Five" sound?

4 ★★☆ **Write present perfect continuous questions.**

0 `e` why / she / cry
Why has she been crying?

1 ☐ how long / she / speak / to the teacher
_____?

2 ☐ how long / you / try to call me
_____?

3 ☐ what / you / do
_____?

4 ☐ how long / Bethany / practice / the piano
_____?

5 ★★☆ **Complete the sentences. Use the present perfect continuous of the verbs.**

a She's *been playing* (play) since 10:30.

b I _____ (try) to reach you for two days.

c They _____ (discuss) the exam for an hour.

d We _____ (clean) our room.

e She _____ (feel) sad about her cat.

6 ★★★ **Match the questions in Exercise 4 with the answers in Exercise 5. Write a–d in the boxes.**

> **PRONUNCIATION**
> Strong and weak forms of *been* /biːn/ and /bɪn/
> Go to page 119. 🎧

Present perfect vs. present perfect continuous

→ SB p.53

7 ★☆☆ **Match the sentences.**

0 He's been wearing these jeans for years. `f`

1 He's bought a new pair of jeans. ☐

2 She's been recording since 7 a.m. ☐

3 She's recorded all the songs for her new album. ☐

4 They've been playing all evening. ☐

5 They've played concerts in many countries. ☐

a She's tired and hungry.

b They have fans all over the world.

c But they're too big for him.

d But they haven't played their best song yet.

e She can go home now.

f He needs to buy a new pair.

8 ★★☆ **Complete the sentences. Use the present perfect or present perfect continuous.**

0 We *'ve been practicing* all afternoon.
We *'ve practiced* 20 songs. (practice)

1 We _____ at photos for hours.
We _____ at all my albums! (look)

2 She _____ 50 messages today!
She _____ emails since eight o'clock. (write)

3 We _____ to songs all evening.
We _____ to five albums. (listen)

4 They _____ the guitar since 2015.
They _____ a lot of concerts. (play)

5 She _____ 300 pictures.
She _____ for many years. (paint)

9 ★★★ **Write questions with *How long* and the present perfect or present perfect continuous.**

0 you / play / the piano
How long have you been playing the piano ?

1 he / know / Greg
_____ ?

2 they / play / in a band
_____ ?

3 you / have / your guitar
_____ ?

4 she / listen / to music
_____ ?

5 they / be / teachers
_____ ?

6 we / live / in this house
_____ ?

10 ★★★ **Complete the questions. Use the correct form of the verbs in the list.**

be | hear | ~~know~~ | play | study

0 How long _____ *have you known* _____ your best friend?

1 What's your favorite sport and how long
_____ it?

2 What class are you in now and how long
_____ in it?

3 How long _____ English?

4 What's the most interesting information you
_____ today?

11 ★★★ **Write your answers to the questions in Exercise 10.**

0 _____

1 _____

2 _____

3 _____

4 _____

GET IT *RIGHT!*

Present perfect continuous vs. past continuous

Learners sometimes use the past continuous when the present perfect continuous is required.

✓ I've **been looking** for a new phone since last week.

✗ I ~~was looking~~ for a new phone since last week.

Complete the sentences with the correct form of the verbs.

0 Over the last few weeks I *'ve been training* (train) for the race.

1 We _____ (eat) breakfast when we heard the news.

2 Nathan _____ (wait) to see the latest *Star Wars* movie for months.

3 Heidi _____ (work) there last year, but she left in December.

4 My brothers _____ (play) the violin for two years.

5 They _____ (get) this discount for the last three years.

6 You left the meeting because your phone _____ (ring).

VOCABULARY
Making music
→ SB p.50

1 ⭐☆☆ **Complete the text with the words in the list.**

> started a band | wrote / songs and lyrics
> recorded / single | download | played gigs
> entered the charts | released | went on / tour

When Mick Jagger ⁰ ___started a band___ called
The Rolling Stones in 1962 with a few friends, he had no
idea how successful they would become. The Stones
¹ _____ their first _____ ,
Come On, a song by the singer Chuck Berry, and
² _____ it on June 7, 1963. They never
performed it when they ³ _____ because
it wasn't "their" song. But their fans found out about
the record and so many people bought it that it
⁴ _____ in the UK and went to number
21. Of course, in those days, fans had to go to record
stores; they couldn't just ⁵ _____ music
from the internet! Mick Jagger and Keith Richards
⁶ _____ a lot of _____
_____ that became very famous.
In 1964, The Rolling Stones ⁷ _____ their
first _____ of the US. When they came
back, they had their first number one hit in the UK,
It's All Over Now.

Musical instruments
→ SB p.53

2 ⭐☆☆ **Put the letters in order to make musical instruments.**

1 The _____drums_____ (sdmur) and the
_____ (sabs aitugr) are responsible for
the rhythm in a band.

2 The _____ (rmutpte) and the
_____ (nxohpasoe) are wind
instruments.

3 _____ (ysedbaokr) are electronic
instruments similar to a _____ (iaopn).

4 The _____ (linvoi) and the
_____ (griuat) are both examples of
string instruments.

3 ⭐⭐☆ **Check (✓) the sentences that are true for you. Correct the ones that aren't.**

1 I never listen to jazz. ☐
_____

2 I prefer pop to rock. ☐
_____

3 I like songs with good melodies. ☐
_____

4 I don't really like rap. ☐
_____

5 I never listen to the lyrics of a song. ☐
_____

WordWise: Phrasal verbs with *out*
→ SB p.51

4 ⭐☆☆ Ⓒircle the correct answers.

0 We need help. Who could ___ this out for us?
　A come　　　Ⓒ sort
　B start　　　D go

1 I'm afraid I'm ___ out of ideas. I'm not sure what to do.
　A coming　　C sorting
　B running　　D finding

2 I love ___ out with my friends.
　A finding　　C sorting
　B starting　　D going

3 My cousin ___ out writing for the local newspaper. Now he's a journalist on TV.
　A started　　C sorted
　B found　　　D went

4 Nobody saw what happened, so it's difficult for the police to ___ out the truth.
　A come　　　C go
　B run　　　　D find

5 They haven't had a new song for two years, but their new album should ___ out soon.
　A sort　　　C go
　B find　　　D come

5 ⭐⭐☆ **Match the questions with the answers.**

0 Why won't you join us at the movies tonight? [c]
1 We have a real problem with this. ☐
2 When did this book come out? ☐
3 What was your brother's first job? ☐
4 Can I talk to Jenny? ☐
5 What if your dad finds out about it? ☐

a I can't remember. I bought it a long time ago.
b Well, he won't be happy, that's for sure.
c I've run out of money. I just can't afford to go.
d Sorry. She's gone out with her sisters.
e Oh, don't worry. I'm sure we'll sort it out.
f He started out as a drummer.

6 ⭐⭐⭐ **Answer the questions so they are true for you.**

1 How many times a week do you go out?
_____

2 Are any of your friends good at sorting out problems? How do they do it?
_____

3 Do you watch new movies as soon as they come out?
_____

4 Does your phone often run out of battery?
_____

REFERENCE

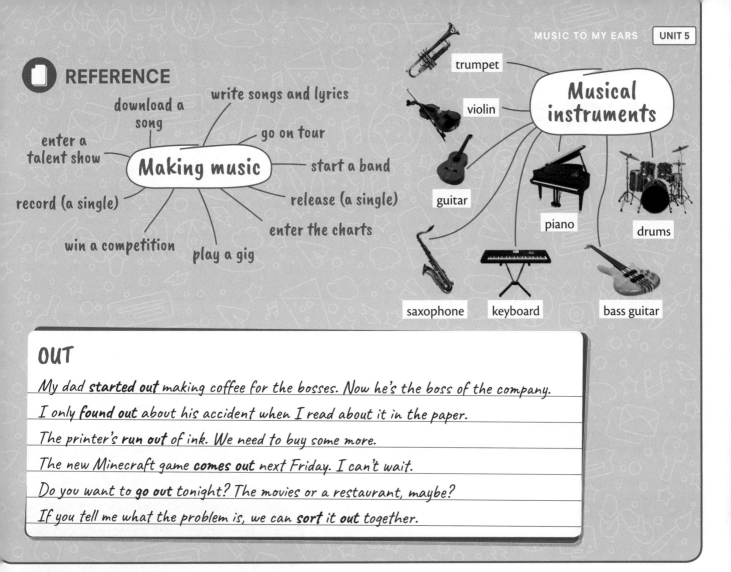

Making music
- download a song
- write songs and lyrics
- enter a talent show
- go on tour
- start a band
- record (a single)
- release (a single)
- enter the charts
- win a competition
- play a gig

Musical instruments
- trumpet
- violin
- guitar
- piano
- drums
- saxophone
- keyboard
- bass guitar

OUT

My dad **started out** making coffee for the bosses. Now he's the boss of the company.

I only **found out** about his accident when I read about it in the paper.

The printer's **run out** of ink. We need to buy some more.

The new Minecraft game **comes out** next Friday. I can't wait.

Do you want to **go out** tonight? The movies or a restaurant, maybe?

If you tell me what the problem is, we can **sort** it **out** together.

VOCABULARY *EXTRA*

1 Circle the correct words.

1 The band is in the studio *performing* / *recording* their album.

2 Lewis Capaldi has many hit *songs* / *dances*.

3 My favorite singer is performing *direct* / *live* on TV tonight.

4 It isn't easy to make a great *album* / *concert*.

5 I really like this group, but I wish they would record some original songs, not just *covers* / *lyrics*.

6 You need a good internet connection to *sing* / *stream* music on your phone.

2 Complete the sentences with the words in the list.

album | covers | live | singles | song | streaming | ~~studio~~

1 Fine Feathers is in the _____studio_____ and they're recording an _____ , *Wind Songs*.

2 They're playing a concert in their hometown so their fans can see them perform _____ . They're going to play some new songs and some well-known _____ .

3 They have a hit _____ , *Bad News*, and it's top of the _____ chart. I keep _____ it on my phone – it's such a good song!

49

A HIDDEN STAR

A young man dreams of a career in music. He gets a chance to record two albums, but they don't sell. For many years, he lives on very little money. He has no idea that in the meantime his songs have become extremely popular in other countries, and that his fans believe he's dead.

It sounds like a fairy tale, but it isn't. It's an incredible but true story and this is only the half of it.

Sixto Rodriguez was the son of Mexican immigrants to the US. He released his first album, *Cold Fact*, in 1970, and his second, *Coming from Reality*, a year later. But nobody bought his music, so he had to do all kinds of jobs to earn enough to support him and his family. Life was hard.

In the meantime, his music was becoming a huge success in three countries on the other side of the world: Australia, New Zealand, and in particular, South Africa. There, Rodriguez was a huge star, more popular than The Rolling Stones. But people were saying he was dead and he himself had no idea about the success of his music.

Then, finally, in December 1994, 24 years after he released *Cold Fact,* a young South African fan named Stephen "Sugar" Segerman and Craig Bartholomew, a journalist, decided to find out more about Rodriguez. They started a website called The Great Rodriguez Hunt and they organized for a photo of his face to be put on milk cartons in the US with the question "Have you seen this man?" Rodriguez's daughter saw one and the rest is rock history.

In March 1998, he was invited on a big tour across South Africa. Rodriguez played six concerts all over the country, in stadiums filled with thousands of young people who knew every word to every one of his songs.

Malik Bendjelloul, a Swedish filmmaker, made a documentary called *Searching for Sugar Man*. The movie told the story of how Segerman and Bartholomew tried to find out if Rodriguez was still alive and how they found him. When the movie got a nomination for an Oscar, the director asked Rodriguez to come to the ceremony, but he refused because he was afraid all the attention would be on him and not the filmmakers. Although the movie has helped to make his music successful around the world, Rodriguez doesn't have a rock star lifestyle. He's been living in the same simple house in Detroit for 40 years and he doesn't have a car, a cell phone, or a TV.

📖 READING

1 Read the article quickly. Complete the fact file.

FACTFILE

Name: ⁰ *Sixto Rodriguez*

Album titles: ¹ _____

² _____

First concert tour (date): ³ _____

Country (of the concert tour): ⁴ _____

2 Read the article again. Mark the sentences T (true) or F (false). Correct the false information.

0 Sixto Rodriguez was born in the US, but his parents were Brazilian. ☐ F
His parents were Mexican.

1 A lot of people knew his music in South Africa. ☐
_____

2 His daughter put a picture of him on milk cartons. ☐
_____

3 Twenty-four years after *Cold Fact*, he played in front of thousands of fans in South Africa. ☐
_____

4 The fans in South Africa knew all of the lyrics of his songs. ☐
_____

5 He has recently made a movie about his life. ☐
_____

3 When she saw the ad, Rodriguez's daughter called Stephen "Sugar" Segerman. Use your imagination to write the first six lines of that phone call.

Daughter *Hello, is this Stephen Segerman?*

Segerman _____

Daughter _____

Segerman _____

Daughter _____

Segerman _____

4 CRITICAL THINKING **Put the events in Rodriguez's life in the correct order.**

☐ **A** Two music fans found Rodriguez in the US.

☐ **B** His music became famous all over the world.

☐ 1 **C** Rodriguez made two albums.

☐ **D** He did a concert tour in South Africa.

☐ **E** He was a famous musician in New Zealand, Australia, and South Africa.

☐ **F** There was a movie about him.

☐ **G** He did ordinary jobs and didn't earn much.

☐ **H** People thought Rodriguez was dead.

DEVELOPING { *Writing*

A magazine article

1 INPUT **Read the article quickly and answer the questions.**

0 What's the singer's real name?
Her real name is Ella Marija Lani Yelich-O'Connor.

1 Where did she grow up?
_____

2 What do experts think of her?
_____
_____

3 What does the writer think of her?
_____
_____
_____

Ruling the world

A In 2013, a song called "Royals" made a young singer named Lorde famous all over the world. Lorde's real name is Ella Marija Lani Yelich-O'Connor and she grew up in New Zealand. <u>She has been working in the music industry since she won a talent show at the age of 12.</u>

B <u>Ever since Lorde appeared on TV screens for the first time, critics have been praising her fantastic voice.</u> She has an incredible feel for music and a unique talent for writing lyrics. She says her love for words has been as important as her love for music and both have helped her to become a star.

C Lorde is still very young. <u>She became a star when she was 17</u>, and has had a number of successful songs since then. *Tennis Court* came out in the UK just after the Wimbledon Tennis Championship in 2013. She released her second album, *Melodrama*, in 2017 and started a world concert tour.

D I have been fascinated by Lorde's music and her personality since I first saw her in a video. Her songs make me happy and I love singing along to them. If you don't know Lorde, listen to some of her music – you'll love it!

2 **Match the content (1–4) with the paragraphs (A–D).**

☐ **1** the writer's personal opinion
☐ **2** the singer's early life
☐ **3** examples of her music
☐ **4** experts' opinions

3 ANALYZE **Look at the <u>underlined</u> sentences in the text. Find examples of verb forms that refer to …**

A something that happened at a specific time in the past.
She became a star when she was 17.
_____

B something that started in the past, and is still continuing.
_____
_____

C how long something has been happening.
_____
_____

> ✏ **WRITING TIP:**
> **a magazine article**
>
> • Think of an interesting title to attract the readers' attention.
> • Start with an interesting opening line or a direct question to the reader.
> • Organize your text in paragraphs.
> • In the last paragraph, give your opinion and/or make a suggestion of something the reader should do.

4 PLAN **You are going to write an article about a singer or a musician alive today.**

1 Choose a singer or musician.
2 Research the information in Exercise 2 points 2–4 about the singer or musician.
3 Use your notes to write a plan. Use the Writing tip to help you.

5 PRODUCE **Write an article about the singer or musician in about 200 words. Use your plan from Exercise 4.**

 **LISTENING**

1 🔊 5.02 **Listen to the conversations and answer the questions.**

Conversation 1

0 What do Tony's friends like that he doesn't?
Listening to music while doing other things.

1 Why can't he listen to music while he's doing something else?

_____

2 When does he like to listen to music?

_____

Conversation 2

3 How does Rachel feel about music?

_____

4 Do her teachers allow her to listen to music during class?

_____

5 How does music make her feel?

_____

Conversation 3

6 Where does Ryan find new music?

_____

7 What are his favorite types of music?

_____

8 Does he listen to music when he works?

_____

DIALOGUE

2 🔊 5.02 **Match the questions with the answers. Then listen again and check.**

0 Why's that? — d

1 So, don't you ever listen to music? — ☐

2 Does it relax you? — ☐

3 Could you live without music? — ☐

4 Do you dance a lot? — ☐

5 When do you listen to that? — ☐

a Yeah, it helps me see pictures.

b Not as often as I'd like to.

c Well, when I need to concentrate.

d Because I can't concentrate on both things.

e No, I don't think I could.

f Of course I do! I like music.

PHRASES FOR FLUENCY → SB p.54

3 🔊 5.03 **Put the conversation in the correct order. Then listen and check.**

☐ Emily   It's The Fallen – they're playing in the town hall on Saturday.

☐ Emily   Why don't we invite Yuri to come along?

1 Emily   Charlie, Charlie!

☐ Emily   Why not? He loves them.

☐ Emily   Well, if you say so. It's just me and you, then.

☐ Emily   Yes, really. I've already gotten my ticket. I can't wait! It's going to be the show of the year.

☐ Charlie   Tell me about it. They're my favorite band. I'm definitely going, too.

☐ Charlie   Yuri? No way.

☐ Charlie   What's up, Emily?

☐ Charlie   What?! Really?

☐ Charlie   Listen, there's no point in trying to change my mind. Yuri and I … well, we just don't like each other. I'd rather not invite him.

4 **Complete the conversations with the phrases in the list.**

> if you say so | there's no point in | I can't wait
> no way | tell me about it | what's up

0 A Stephen King is the best writer in the world.
   B _____If you say so_____ . I prefer Suzanne Collins.

1 A I've told her again and again that she's wrong.
   B _____ talking to her. She just won't listen.

2 A Wow, that class was boring.
   B _____ . I almost fell asleep twice!

3 A Let's climb that tree.
   B _____ . That's far too dangerous.

4 A Hey, Tom. I need to talk to you.
   B OK, Jules. _____ ?

5 A I'm so happy it'll be summer soon.
   B Me, too. _____ to go swimming.

B1 Preliminary for Schools

1 🔊 **5.04** **For each question, write the correct answer in the gap.**

Write **one** or **two words**, or a **number**, or a **date** or a **time**.

You will hear a teacher talking about a school trip to a museum.

Museum of Popular Music

The building was once a [1]_____ .

The main exhibition is about music from
[2]_____ to the present.

A special exhibition has a display of
musicians' [3]_____ .

There is a 30-minute film about the
history of [4]_____ .

You can see what it's like in a
professional [5]_____ .

The museum gives students a gift if they
do a [6]_____ about the exhibition.

EXAM GUIDE: LISTENING PART 3

In B1 Preliminary for Schools Listening Part 3, you listen to one person speaking about something. While you listen, you have to complete some notes. There are six gaps and you have to write one or two words, or a date or a time in each gap.

Before you listen:
- Read through the notes.
- For each gap, think about the type of word/s you expect to hear, for example: name, number, date, time.

While you listen:
- Remember you will hear the information in the same order as the notes.
- Focus on the information you need to complete the notes.
- Start completing the gaps when you listen for the first time.
- The second time you listen, check your answers and any gaps you were unable to complete the first time you listened.

6 NO PLANET B

▶ 17

Grammar rap!

GRAMMAR

will (not), may (not), might (not) for prediction → SB p.58

1 ★☆☆ **Match the sentences with the pictures.**

0 Mom won't be happy when she sees her car. `F`

1 Mom will be happy when she sees her car. ☐

2 Don't eat it all. You'll get sick. ☐

3 Don't eat it. It might be poisonous. ☐

4 She may not finish her book tonight. ☐

5 She won't finish her book tonight. ☐

2 ★★☆ **Complete the sentences. Use *will* or *won't* and the verbs in the list.**

| ~~be~~ | believe | cost | get | like | remember |

0 He's grown a lot. He __will be__ taller than me soon.

1 I don't know how much the tickets _____ .

2 Wow! They _____ me when I tell them!

3 Listen carefully. Otherwise you _____ what I tell you.

4 Don't worry. I _____ there as soon as I can.

5 The cake is for Amanda. I'm sure she _____ it.

3 ★★☆ Circle **the correct words.**

0 I'm nervous. Mom (might) / won't get angry.

1 Wait there. I *'ll / might* be two minutes.

2 I don't know the answer. Who *won't / might* know?

3 Both teams are good. I have no idea who *will / won't* win.

4 It's getting late. We *may / may not* miss the train.

5 I'll tell you, but you *might / won't* believe me.

6 They probably *won't / might not* come at all.

4 ★★★ **Write predictions with suitable modal verbs.**

0 there / only be / electric cars / 20 years from now (certainty)

There will only be electric cars 20 years from now.

1 we / visit / the US / next summer (possibility)

_____

2 I / watch / a movie / in English / next week (possibility)

_____

3 My friends / not see / a game / on Sunday (certainty)

_____

4 next month / there / be / a lot of rain (possibility)

_____

5 Samuel / go / to college / one day (certainty)

_____

6 Maria / watch TV / tonight (possibility)

_____

5 ★★★ **Check (✓) the predictions in Exercise 4 that are true for you. Change the others so that they are true for you.**

1 ☐ _____
2 ☐ _____
3 ☐ _____
4 ☐ _____
5 ☐ _____
6 ☐ _____

6 ★★★ **Write six sentences about the future of your country. Use *will, won't, might (not),* and *may (not).***

1 _____
2 _____
3 _____
4 _____
5 _____
6 _____

First conditional; *unless* in first conditional sentences → SB p.61

7 ★☆☆ Circle the correct words.

0 If I(see)/ 'll see her again, I'll tell her to call you.

1 We won't go on vacation if Dad *is / will be* still sick.

2 If you *won't / don't* talk about it, nobody will know.

3 *Will / Do* they want to come if they hear about the party?

4 If they don't help, their parents *will be / are* angry.

5 If you think carefully, I'm sure you *find / 'll find* a nice present for her.

6 There won't be many people at the game if the weather *gets / will get* worse.

7 If you *won't / don't* keep in touch with your friends, they'll lose interest in you.

8 ★★☆ Match the parts of the sentences.

0 I'll take the train — d

1 Will they come for lunch

2 If you don't tell Tasha about the situation,

3 I won't call you

4 If they don't want to come to your party,

5 She'll only buy the phone

6 If people hear how much the tickets are,

7 Unless the teacher gives us really difficult homework,

a I'll finish it before seven o'clock.

b you'll have to accept their decision.

c a lot of them won't go.

d unless Dad gives me a ride.

e if it isn't too expensive.

f how will she know?

g unless I change my plans.

h if we invite them?

9 ★★☆ Complete the text. Use the correct form of the verbs in the list.

be | be | go | invite | miss | not let | not pass

Dear Diary,

Not a great day today. Had a test in French. Unless I'm totally wrong, my score ⁰ _____won't be_____ very good. If I ¹ _____ , I don't know what I'll do. My parents ² _____ me go to the movies with Brandon tomorrow unless I pass. If I tell Brandon I can't go to the movies with him, he ³ _____ someone else. If he ⁴ _____ with someone else, I ⁵ _____ a movie I'd love to see. But what if I wait and tell my parents later? Well, who knows how they'll react? I think that unless I come up with a good idea, I ⁶ _____ in trouble whatever I do. Well, one thing's for sure: next time I'll prepare better for my French test.

10 ★★★ Write first conditional questions. Then match them with the answers.

0 rain / what / you do
If it rains, what will you do?
_____

1 watch TV tonight / what / you / watch
_____

2 what / you / buy / get / birthday money
_____

3 feel hungry / at break / what / you / eat
_____

4 what / you / do / not pass / the exam
_____

5 what / you / do / lose / your phone
_____

a I'll ask my mom for a new one.

b That won't happen!

c Nothing. I think I'll save the money.

d I'll stay at home.

e I'll watch a movie.

f A sandwich or some cookies.

11 ★★★ Answer three of the questions in Exercise 10 about you.

GET IT RIGHT!

First conditional tenses

Learners sometimes use *will* instead of the present tense in the first conditional.

✓ I will be pleased if they **like** it.

✗ I will be pleased if they ~~will~~ like it.

Correct the sentences.

0 I'll let you know if we'll be late.
I'll let you know if we're late.

1 If we have some help, there isn't a problem.
_____

2 I will wear a coat if it will be cold.
_____

3 They'll understand if you'll explain it.
_____

4 Will he go if the meeting will be at 7:00?
_____

5 If it won't rain, they'll have a picnic.
_____

PRONUNCIATION
/f/, /v/, and /b/ consonant sounds
Go to page 119. 🎧

55

AZ VOCABULARY
The environment
→ SB p.58

1 ★☆☆ **Write the words under the photos.**

> flood | litter | melting ice | pollution
> recycling | trash | ~~smog~~

1 ____smog____ , _____

2 _____

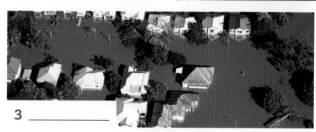

3 _____

4 _____ , _____ , _____

2 ★★☆ **Match the parts of the sentences.**

0 Many people think we need stricter ⬜ g

1 Water bottles are an example of ⬜

2 If global warming continues, many glaciers ⬜

3 Some parts of the world don't get enough rain, ⬜

4 Many animals, birds, and insects will
become extinct ⬜

5 Recycling paper means ⬜

6 This river's water is very clean – there doesn't seem ⬜

7 To help the environment, we should avoid ⬜

a while others have frequent floods.

b will melt. This will be bad for our planet.

c to be any pollution here.

d single-use plastics.

e wasting natural resources, such as electricity.

f if we don't do something to protect them.

g laws to protect the environment.

h we don't need to cut down so many trees.

Verbs to talk about energy
→ SB p.61

3 ★★☆ Ⓒircle the correct option: A, B, or C.

0 If you reuse something, ___
  A you throw it away.
  B you charge it.
  Ⓒ you use it again.

1 Turning the lights off ___
  A destroys forests.
  B saves energy.
  C wastes energy.

2 It's better to disconnect electrical appliances
  from their ___
  A litter.
  B power source.
  C standby.

3 Taking a long shower ___ a lot of water.
  A wastes
  B saves
  C recycles

4 If you ___ electronic gadgets on standby,
  you waste electricity.
  A save
  B disconnect
  C leave

5 You should disconnect your phone as soon as it is ___ .
  A charged
  B wasted
  C reused

6 You shouldn't ___ plastic, paper, glass, or metal.
  Recycle it!
  A throw away
  B reuse
  C disconnect

4 ★★★ **Answer the questions.**

1 What do you think is the biggest threat to our
  environment and why?

  _____

  _____

2 How do you feel when you see someone throw litter
  away in the street?

  _____

  _____

3 Have you ever told somebody not to waste paper /
  plastic / water / energy? How did they react?

  _____

  _____

4 What positive examples do you know of people
  caring for the environment?

  _____

  _____

REFERENCE

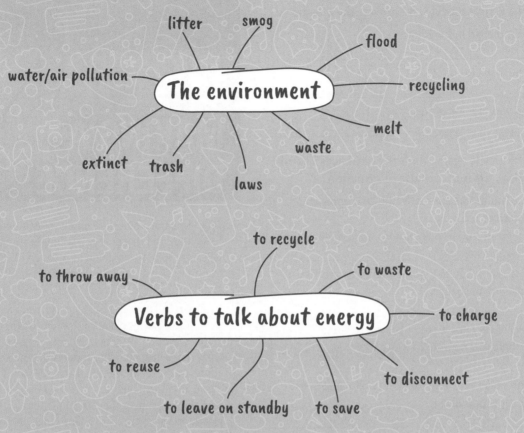

VOCABULARY *EXTRA*

1   Match the words with the definitions.

0 generate energy	`d`	**a** keep to use later
1 upcycle furniture	☐	**b** use less
2 damage the environment	☐	**c** make sure it keeps existing
3 store energy	☐	**d** produce
4 preserve the environment	☐	**e** have a bad effect on
5 reduce energy	☐	**f** make nicer using old materials

2   Complete the sentences with the correct form of the verbs in the list.

> ~~damage~~ | generate | preserve | reduce | store | upcycle

0 The environment is being _____*damaged*_____ by the amount of energy we all use.

1 We have _____ an old sofa and it has changed the look of the whole living room!

2 We must try harder to _____ the environment or some animal species will disappear soon.

3 _____ energy from the sun or wind will help us to prevent climate change.

4 By _____ our energy consumption, we can help the environment.

5 Governments need to think of ways to _____ the energy that solar power produces.

3   Think of an item of furniture in your house that you would like to upcycle. What would you do to it? Write sentences.

_____

_____

_____

📖 READING

1 Read the article quickly and answer the questions.

1 Who is the girl in the photo?

_____

2 Where is she from?

_____

3 What was her first protest?

_____

2 Read the article again. Mark the sentences **T** (true) or **F** (false). Correct the false information.

0 Greta Thunberg's interest in the environment only started recently. [F]

Her interest in the environment started when she
was eight years old.

1 She was surprised that adults were very worried about climate change. ☐

_____

2 Weeks of very hot weather proved to Greta that there was no time to waste. ☐

_____

3 It didn't take very long for Greta's Climate Strike to become popular. ☐

_____

4 Greta believes if we do something immediately, we might be able to save the planet. ☐

_____

5 When she speaks, she doesn't like to scare people with facts about climate change. ☐

_____

6 Greta believes that teenagers are too young to make a difference. ☐

_____

3 Imagine you have the chance to speak to world leaders. What are you going to speak about and why? Write a short text (50–100 words).

I am going to speak about …

4 `CRITICAL THINKING` Find a sentence, or part of a sentence, in each paragraph that sums up the writer's ideas.

Paragraph 1
Here's an example of a young person who
made a lot of people pay attention.

Paragraph 2

_____

Paragraph 3

_____

Paragraph 4

_____

Paragraph 5

_____

GRETA: MAKING A DIFFERENCE

1 Imagine you feel strongly about something and you want to talk about it. You might think that no one will want to hear what you have to say. Well, here's an example of a young person who made a lot of people pay attention.

2 Greta Thunberg is a teenager from Sweden. She was eight years old when she first heard about global warming at school. She was very worried about what she heard, but what shocked her most was that adults didn't seem to think it was serious. They weren't doing anything about it. From then on, she couldn't stop thinking about the danger of climate change. She persuaded her parents to change their lifestyle: the family became vegan and started growing their own vegetables. They traveled by train instead of plane and changed to solar energy in their home.

3 The summer of 2018 was particularly hot in Europe with more extreme weather than usual. Greta knew it was time for action. When workers have strikes, they refuse to work because they want better pay. When Greta had a Climate Strike, she refused to go to school because she wanted a better world. She wanted everyone to understand two things: climate change was real and it was serious. One Friday, instead of going to school, she biked to the Swedish Parliament. She sat alone all the first day, but the next day, people started joining her protest after reading her posters about global warming. This small protest led to the first of many global Climate Strikes in December of 2018, by more than 20,000 students in over 270 cities around the world.

4 Greta, now known internationally, began traveling around Europe to speak at important meetings. Her message is always very clear: unless you do something now, you will destroy our future. She told world leaders at a conference in Switzerland, "I don't want you to feel hopeful. I want you to panic […] And then I want you to act." At a United Nations climate change meeting in Poland, she said, "The year 2078, I will celebrate my 75th birthday. If I have children, maybe they will spend that day with me. Maybe they will ask me about you. Maybe they will ask why."

5 Greta's actions have made adults and young people take action around the world. She has already won many international awards and she might win more. Greta Thunberg has shown that young people can make a difference if they're brave enough to talk about the things they believe in.

An article about an issue

1 **INPUT** **Read the extracts quickly and match them with the titles.**

1 Climate change ☐   **2** The problem with pollution ☐   **3** Deforestation ☐   **4** Not enough water ☐

A In conclusion, if the level of the oceans keeps rising, many small islands will disappear. People and animals will die. Unfortunately, this really will all happen unless we change the way we live. So please join me and write to organizations and politicians to ask them to support the environment. ☐

B In many parts of the world, people don't have enough water. When people can't find enough water or use water that is clean, they will catch diseases more easily. This is a big problem in hot and tropical countries. In this essay, I will explain what we can do to make sure that people all around the world have enough water. ☐

C We need to make sure that there are enough trains and buses so that people can travel on public transportation. We also need to encourage people to walk and cycle more and use their cars less because this will mean that we will have less pollution in our towns and cities. ☐

D That is why we must introduce new laws to protect forests and rainforests. Big companies earn millions from selling wood, so they should give some of the money they earn to save rainforests. If they don't do this, they should have to pay a fine and the people who own these companies should go to prison. ☐

2 **Write (B) beginning, (M) middle, or (C) conclusion next to each extract.**

3 **ANALYZE** **Read the phrases 0–6 and put them in the correct column.**

0 Millions of trees are cut down every year.
1 Unless people do something now, it might be too late.
2 We must encourage people to stop driving their cars.
3 Every year, we lose large areas of forest.
4 Some people can't find clean water to drink or wash in.
5 If we don't reduce pollution now, climate change will get worse.
6 First, we need to learn about how many countries will lose land through climate change.

Description of a problem	Say what will happen	Suggested action
0	_____	_____
_____	_____	_____

4 **Match each sentence with the extract it could come from. Then complete the sentences with the linking words in the list.**

> that is why | if | unless | so | ~~because~~

0 These animals are endangered _*because*_ the ocean levels are rising.   [A]
1 Every year, more trees are cut down. _____ we need to take some real action now. ☐
2 Climate change will continue _____ we all change the way we live now. ☐
3 We need to build more wells _____ that everyone can drink fresh, clean water. ☐
4 We need to let people know what will happen _____ everybody uses their car all the time. ☐

✏ WRITING TIP: an article about an issue

- Give your article a title.
- Make sure your article has a beginning, a middle, and a conclusion.
- Use linking words to connect your arguments.
- Describe the issue clearly and simply.
- Explain the possible future results.
- Suggest ways we can help.

5 **PLAN** **You are going to write an article about a global environmental issue. Plan your article and make notes. Use the Writing tip to help you.**

- Choose a global environmental issue.
- Describe the problem.
- Explain what will or might happen if nothing changes.
- Make suggestions to solve it.
- Use the Writing tip to help you.

6 **PRODUCE** **Write an article in about 200 words. Use your plan from Exercise 5.**

🎧 LISTENING

1 🔊 6.03 **Listen to the conversations and match them with the photos.**

A ☐

B ☐

C ☐

2 🔊 6.03 **Listen again. Circle the correct answers.**

0 Why is Amelia excited?
- **A** She's going to visit a nature area.
- **B** She's going to finish her project.
- **C** Her class is going on a trip to the zoo.

1 What's Toby's opinion of the decision?
- **A** He doesn't think it's a good idea.
- **B** He isn't very enthusiastic.
- **C** He's surprised and can't believe it.

2 What are the friends going to do?
- **A** work in a friend's yard.
- **B** make a place cleaner and nicer
- **C** go for a walk by the river

DIALOGUE

3 🔊 6.03 **Match the sentences. Then listen again to check.**

1 Well, to be honest, we didn't win. ☐
2 Come on, Toby! Aren't you pleased? ☐
3 We don't have any classes today. ☐
4 Nobody said no, so there'll be about ten of us. ☐
5 We're going to clean all the trash out of the river. ☐

a Wow! That's incredible!
b What a great idea! I'll definitely be there.
c Well, sort of.
d What do you mean? Of course we did.
e Oh really? How come?

4 **Complete the phrases with the missing vowels.**

0 Wh _a_ t _a_ gr_e_ _a_t id_e_ _a_ !
1 Th __ t's __ m __ z __ ng!
2 Th __ t s __ __ nds __ xc __ t __ ng!
3 W __ w!
4 __ h, r __ __ __ lly?
5 H __ w __ xc __ t __ ng!
6 C __ __ __ l!
7 __ ncr __ d __ bl __ !

5 **Write two short conversations about people telling their friends some exciting news.**

Train to TH!NK

Recognizing different text types

6 **Read the extracts and write the text types. Check your answers using page 60 of the Student's Book.**

0 Hi Jay, Gr8 you'll come over to my place on Sunday. Got some cool videos to show you. Love, B
Text message

1 Pop in and check out our vegetables – grown by local farmers and brought to you daily by us.

_____

2 Monday: another cool day at school. Science project interesting, working with Lisa. Tomorrow track and field competition.

_____

3 He opened his eyes. He had no idea where he was, but he knew the place was dangerous.

_____

4 Joel, please feed the cat. Food's in the fridge. See you tonight, Mom

_____

5 A spokesman for SpaceLive said to reporters on Tuesday that the company was thinking of sending plants to the moon.

_____

B1 Preliminary for Schools

WRITING
Part 1: Email

1 **You must answer this question. Write your answer in about 100 words.**

Read this email from your English-speaking friend, Riley, and the notes you have made.

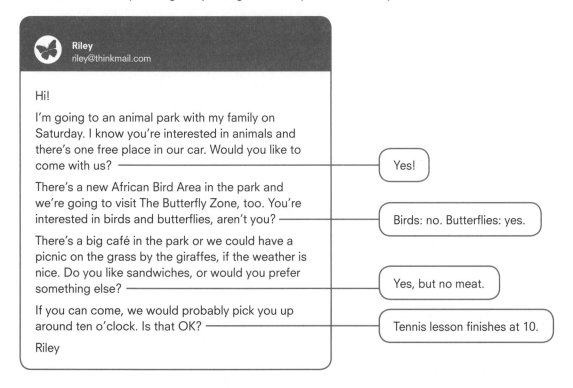

Riley
riley@thinkmail.com

Hi!

I'm going to an animal park with my family on Saturday. I know you're interested in animals and there's one free place in our car. Would you like to come with us? —— Yes!

There's a new African Bird Area in the park and we're going to visit The Butterfly Zone, too. You're interested in birds and butterflies, aren't you? —— Birds: no. Butterflies: yes.

There's a big café in the park or we could have a picnic on the grass by the giraffes, if the weather is nice. Do you like sandwiches, or would you prefer something else? —— Yes, but no meat.

If you can come, we would probably pick you up around ten o'clock. Is that OK? —— Tennis lesson finishes at 10.

Riley

Write your email to Riley, using all the notes.

SUGGESTED PLAN:

* Thank your friend for the invitation.
* Accept and explain why.
* Say you don't like birds, but you like butterflies, and why.
* Say you like sandwiches, but that you don't eat meat.
* Say you have a tennis lesson until 10 and ask if that is OK.
* Finish with a friendly phrase.

EXAM GUIDE: WRITING PART 1

In B1 Preliminary for Schools Writing Part 1, you have to write an answer to an email. There are four notes and you must include <u>all</u> of these in your answer.

* Read the instructions carefully.
* Then read the email and the notes.
* Make a plan before you start writing.
* Remember to answer all the questions, not just one or two.
* Remember who you're writing to and use appropriate language (formal or informal).

CONSOLIDATION

🎧 LISTENING

1 🔊 6.04 **Listen to the conversation. Check (✓) A, B, or C.**

1 Who chose the name of the band?
- **A** Alice ☐
- **B** Joe ☐
- **C** Ben ☐

2 What instrument does Joe play in the band?
- **A** keyboard ☐
- **B** guitar ☐
- **C** drums ☐

3 What instrument does Tamsin play?
- **A** trumpet ☐
- **B** saxophone ☐
- **C** violin ☐

2 🔊 6.04 **Listen again and answer the questions.**

0 Why is the band called The Green Warriors?
to show that they care about the environment

1 What does Ben do in the band?
_____

2 What do Jessica and Lucy play in the band?
_____

3 How long has Tamsin been playing the saxophone?
_____

4 Where does the band practice?
_____

 GRAMMAR

3 Circle **the correct words.**

I've ⁰*worked* / *been working* at the local nature reserve for three months. I spend half my time at the reserve and half my time visiting schools. I've ¹*already visited* / *been visiting* about 20 schools in the local area. I think it's very important to talk to teenagers. If they ²*don't* / *won't* learn how to love the environment, there ³*isn't* / *won't be* much future for our world. One of the projects I've ⁴*worked* / *been working* on for the last few months is trying to stop the town from building hundreds of new houses. Unless we ⁵*do* / *don't do* something to stop it, it ⁶*will* / *won't* cause serious problems for the local wildlife because they want to build them on an important site for many rare birds. I've ⁷*already written* / *been writing* about 30 letters to the local politician, but so far he hasn't ⁸*replied* / *been replying* to me.

4 **Complete the sentences with the correct present perfect or present perfect continuous form of the verbs.**

0 Jane Cooper ___*has been*___ (be) a famous writer for a long time.

1 She _____ (write) over 30 novels now.

2 She _____ (write) novels for many years.

3 She _____ (make) a lot of money.

4 Thousands of people _____ (send) her letters.

5 She _____ (reply) to all of them!

6 Since last month, she _____ (think) about her next novel.

7 But she still _____ (not decide) what the new novel will be about.

🅰️ VOCABULARY

5 **Match the parts of the sentences.**

0 Marty James started writing — *g*
1 He started ☐
2 They played their first ☐
3 The band entered ☐
4 And they won ☐
5 For their prize they got the chance ☐
6 The song was ☐
7 It soon entered ☐
8 Next month the band is going ☐

a a talent show.
b to record an album.
c downloaded over 200,000 times.
d on a national tour.
e gig in the school auditorium.
f the competition.
g songs when he was 12.
h a band a year later.
i the pop charts.

6 **Read the pamphlet and complete the words. The first letters are given.**

THREE SIMPLE WAYS TO MAKE A DIFFERENCE:

› ⁰S*ave*_____ your plastic bags and ¹r_____ them next time you go shopping – don't ²t_____ them ³a_____ .

› ⁴R_____ your trash – sort out the plastic from the paper and the glass.

› ⁵D_____ electronics at night. Don't leave them on ⁶s_____ . It just ⁷w_____ power.

DIALOGUE

7 🔊 **6.05** **Complete the conversation with the phrases in the list. There is one phrase you don't need. Then listen and check.**

> How exciting! | I can't wait. | I'm just a bit upset.
> If you say so | No way. | So, what's the matter?
> There's no point in | ~~What a great idea!~~
> What's up, Jennie?

Jennie Have you heard the news?

Ronan What news?

Jennie We're having a school concert to raise money for the Clean Up Our Air campaign.

Ronan ⁰ *What a great idea!*

Jennie And our band's playing.

Ronan ¹_____

Jennie Isn't it? ²_____

[Two days later]

Ronan ³_____ You don't look very happy.

Jennie It's nothing. ⁴_____

Ronan ⁵_____

Jennie Remember the school concert I told you about the other day? Well, it's been canceled.

Ronan ⁶_____

Jennie Yes, it's true. The principal decided it wasn't a good idea.

Ronan That isn't right. We have to do something. I'm going to talk to him now.

Jennie ⁷_____ trying to change his mind.

📖 READING

8 **Read the article. Mark the sentences T (true) or F (false). Correct the false information.**

0 Kashy Keegan became famous when he wrote his song *This Is My Dream*. ☐F

   Kashy became famous five years later.

1 Five years after he wrote *This Is My Dream*, Kashy decided to put it online. ☐

   _____

2 A Hong Kong TV station wanted to use this song to advertise their shows. ☐

   _____

3 Kashy contacted the TV station and asked to perform in Hong Kong. ☐

   _____

4 People in Hong Kong thought Kashy was famous in his home country. ☐

   _____

Kashy Keegan always wanted to be a pop star and spent years trying to make it happen. In 2007, when he was 22, he wrote what he felt would finally be his big hit, a song called *This Is My Dream*, but it never happened. As the years passed, he started to give up on his musical career. In 2012, he decided to upload the song to a music–sharing website. He hoped someone might like it.

A few months later, he received an email from Universal Music in Hong Kong. They were starting a new TV channel and they wanted to use *This Is My Dream* as the theme tune to one of their shows. Kashy was really excited and made a deal for $5,000.

When the TV station invited Kashy to Hong Kong, hundreds of fans were waiting for him at the airport. Everyone thought he was a big star in the UK, so he explained that back home, no one knew who he was. A little later, Kashy was singing the song live to more than 30,000 screaming fans. After the show, he gave interviews and signed autographs. The next day, he was in all the newspapers and the song went to number one in the charts.

Kashy's pop dream was finally happening! In 2016, he recorded *This is my Dream* in Chinese and released the video on his Vevo channel. He became one of the first European musicians to write and sing a song in Chinese.

✏️ WRITING

9 **Write a short text (about 120–150 words) about your favorite song. Include the following information:**

- who the song is by
- when it first came out
- how popular it became
- what the song is about
- why you like it

7 THE FUTURE IS NOW

Grammar rap! ▶ 20

GRAMMAR
Future forms
→ SB p.68

1 ★☆☆ Complete the rules with the simple present, the present continuous, *be going to*, or *will/won't*.

There are four ways to express the future in English.

1 We often use _____ to make predictions about the future.

2 We often use _____ to talk about future arrangements.

3 We often use _____ to talk about fixed future events.

4 We often use _____ to talk about future plans and intentions.

2 ★☆☆ Complete the sentences with the correct form of the verbs in the list.

arrive | close | finish | ~~leave~~ | open | start

1 The train _____*leaves*_____ New York at 12:40 p.m. and _____ in Boston at 2:50 p.m.

2 The show _____ at 9 p.m. and _____ at 11:15 p.m.

3 Today is Sunday. Tomorrow the café _____ at 8 a.m. and _____ at 7 p.m.

3 ★★☆ Read the sentences. Circle the correct descriptions.

0 The movie starts at nine o'clock.
prediction / (*fixed event*)

1 They're meeting on Saturday.
arrangement / fixed event

2 Your plane arrives at 6 a.m. on Tuesday.
fixed event / prediction

3 My sister's going to study IT in college.
intention / arrangement

4 Joseph and Mia are getting married in June.
arrangement / prediction

5 We won't need phones in the future.
intention / prediction

6 I'm going to act in a movie one day.
fixed event / intention

7 Bradley will be very tall when he's older.
arrangement / prediction

8 My dad's starting his new job next week.
intention / arrangement

9 Our players will win the final easily.
arrangement / prediction

10 We're going to have something healthy for dinner.
intention / arrangement

4 ★★★ Complete the sentences with the correct form of the verbs.

0 Grandma _____*will be*_____ (be) pleased to see you.

1 Tonight, Jo and I _____ (watch) a movie at home.

2 He says he _____ (be) a movie star one day.

3 My exam _____ (be) on Friday next week.

4 I've spoken to Callum and we _____ (go) to the game on Saturday.

5 I think the world _____ (end) with a big bang.

6 My cousin _____ (get) her degree next year.

7 Hurry up! The train _____ (leave) in five minutes.

8 He isn't a bad player, but he _____ (not win) the championship next year.

9 The store _____ (not open) until ten.

10 They're _____ (bring out) a new album next month.

Question tags

→ SB p.71

5 ★★☆ **Complete the conversation with the question tags.**

Ms. Shaw Good afternoon, Sally. Now, you're 18 years old, 0 _aren't you_ ?

Sally No, 19. My birthday was last week.

Ms. Shaw And you live in Philadelphia, 1_____ ?

Sally Yes, when I'm not at the university.

Ms. Shaw But you didn't go to school in Philadelphia, 2_____ ?

Sally No, my parents lived in Boston then.

Ms. Shaw I see. Now you're doing a degree in education, 3_____ ?

Sally Yes, that's right.

Ms. Shaw And you can sing, 4_____ ?

Sally Yes, I sing pretty well.

Ms. Shaw But you can't play the guitar, 5_____ ?

Sally No, I'm afraid not.

Ms. Shaw You have three sisters, 6_____ ?

Sally Yes, and two brothers.

Ms. Shaw You helped organize parties for your sisters, 7_____ ?

Sally Yes, and I take care of my friends' kids sometimes.

Ms. Shaw But you've never had a job before, 8_____ ?

Sally No, but I'd really like this one. I'm sure I'll be good at it.

Ms. Shaw You'll be able to start next month, 9_____ ?

Sally Yes, of course. Does that mean I got the job?

Ms. Shaw Maybe. We'll let you know.

Nor, neither and so

→ SB p.71

6 ★★☆ (Circle) the correct words.

Ms. Shaw I think Sally did very well in her interview.

Manager 0(So)/ Nor do I. She answered the questions very clearly. I liked her!

Ms. Shaw So 1_do / did_ I! She was very impressive.

Manager But I want to see other people.

Ms. Shaw 2_So / Nor_ do I. There's another candidate – his name is Tim. But I haven't read his application form yet.

Manager Neither 3_did / have_ I. But that's OK – I can read it now, quickly.

Ms. Shaw So 4_do / can_ I. But I need a break first.

Manager So 5_am / do_ I. Let's get a cup of coffee.

7 ★★★ **Write Tim's replies.**

Sally I'm trying to get a job for the summer.

Tim 0 _____So am I._____

Sally I've just had an interview.

Tim 1_____

Sally I was really nervous.

Tim 2_____

Sally I didn't sleep well the night before.

Tim 3_____

Sally If I get the job, I'll start next month.

Tim 4_____

Sally But I don't know if I got the job.

Tim 5_____

Sally I don't like waiting for the answer.

Tim 6_____

Sally I won't know the answer until next week.

Tim 7_____

Sally By the way, which job did you apply for?

Tim Children's party organizer. And you?

GET IT RIGHT!

Neither / So do I

Learners sometimes do not use *neither* and *so* when they can be used.

✓ Mike will go to the party and **so** will we.

✗ Mike will go to the party and ~~we will go to the party~~.

Check (✓) the sentences in which the underlined words can be replaced with *neither* or *so*. Rewrite them where possible.

0 I've met Mario and Pablo has met him too. ✓
   I've met Mario and so has Pablo.

1 My mom likes soap operas, but I don't. ☐
   _____

2 Max was there and Elena was there, too. ☐
   _____

3 I can't go to the party and Joe can't go. ☐
   _____

4 We speak French, but our parents don't. ☐
   _____

5 I don't eat meat and Kai doesn't eat it. ☐
   _____

PRONUNCIATION

Intonation in question tags Go to page 120. 🎧

VOCABULARY
Future time expressions 〜 SB p.68

1 ★☆☆ **Put the words in order to make future time expressions.**

0 too / before / long   *before too long*
1 the / next / week / after   _____
2 tomorrow / the / after / day   _____
3 near / the / future / in   _____
4 now / weeks / from / three   _____
5 time / in / years' / two   _____
6 this / later / month   _____

2 ★★☆ **Answer the questions.**

0 What day is it the day after tomorrow?
   The day after tomorrow is Thursday.

1 Where do you think you'll be in ten years' time?
  _____
  _____

2 What do you think will happen later this year?
  _____
  _____

3 Do you think you will go abroad in the near future?
  _____
  _____

4 Do you think you'll get a new phone before too long?
  _____
  _____

5 What do you think you'll be doing five years from now?
  _____
  _____

3 ★★☆ **Circle the correct words.**

0 Some scientists think we will put people on Mars *the day after tomorrow* / (*in the near future.*)
1 Finn is 14 years old, so he'll be able to drive a car *in a few years' time* / *a week from now*.
2 My laptop is really slow. I'll probably get a new one *before too long* / *in four years' time*.
3 Alexa is in Rome this week and she's going to Paris *later this month* / *in a few hours' time*.
4 The date today is the 1st of December. New Year's Day will be *in a month's time* / *the week after next*.
5 Julia is on vacation next week, but she'll be back at work *in two days' time* / *the week after next*.
6 It's March. Kyle was born in September, so his next birthday is *in six months' time* / *in a day's time*.
7 Today is Tuesday. Lyra is taking her driving test on Thursday. That's *later this year* / *in two days' time*.

Arranging a party 〜 SB p.71

4 ★★☆ **Sally got the job as a children's party organizer. Complete the phone conversation with the words in the list.**

> deposit | food | guests | hire | invitations
> organize | ~~permission~~ | room | theme

Mom Hello, Sally. How's the job going?
Sally Fine, thanks! I'm working on a party for a boy who's going to be five in two weeks' time.
Mom What do you have to do?
Sally Well, it's in the community center, so I have to get ⁰___*permission*___ . Then we choose a ¹_____ – Spider-Man or something – and I find out what ²_____ the kids want.
Mom Pizzas, probably! Do you have to ³_____ a cake?
Sally Yes. And the parents draw up a list of ⁴_____ – all the boy's friends – and I send ⁵_____ .
Mom And entertainment?
Sally Yes, they want to ⁶_____ a clown, so I have to pay a ⁷_____ .
Mom It sounds like a lot of work.
Sally Yes, it is. But I love it. I enjoy decorating the ⁸_____ , but the best part is seeing the kids having fun.

WordWise: Phrases with *about* 〜 SB p.69

5 ★★☆ **Complete the conversations with *about* and the words in the list.**

> forget | ~~six~~ | sorry | them
> think | to | you | 75

0 **A** So, are you coming to the movies this evening?
  B Yes. I'll see you at ___*about six*___ o'clock.
1 **A** Will you come with us?
  B I'm not sure, but I'll _____ it.
2 **A** Hey! You're late!
  B Yes, I'm really _____ that.
3 **A** He looks really old.
  B Yes, I think he's _____ .
4 **A** Everyone's going, Dani. What _____ ?
  B No, I don't want to go, thanks.
5 **A** What's wrong? Is your homework hard?
  B It's really hard! I'm _____ go crazy!
6 **A** I'm so sorry I was late yesterday.
  B No problem. Just _____ it, OK?
7 **A** I need help with my project on the Tudors.
  B Sorry – I don't know anything _____ .

 **REFERENCE**

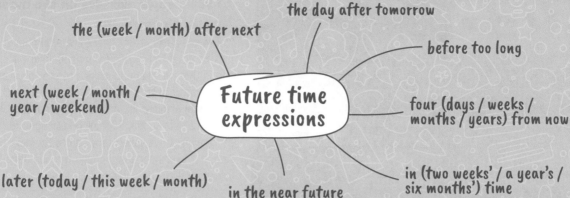

the day after tomorrow

the (week / month) after next

before too long

next (week / month / year / weekend)

Future time expressions

four (days / weeks / months / years) from now

later (today / this week / month)

in the near future

in (two weeks' / a year's / six months') time

ARRANGING A PARTY

to choose a theme

to decorate the room

to draw up a guest list

to get permission

to hire a DJ

to send out invitations

to organize food and drinks

ABOUT

about (ten o'clock / half an hour)

about to (go home)

What about you?

sorry about (that)

forget about (it)

think about (it)

VOCABULARY *EXTRA*

1   Write the words under the photos.

costumes | ~~decorations~~ | entertainment | event | poster

0 ___decorations___ 1 _____ 2 _____ 3 _____ 4 _____

2   Complete the sentences with the words in Exercise 1.

We're going to have an end of term party!

0   Taylor and Daisy are going to **hire the** ___entertainment___ .

1   Sam's going to **design the** _____ .

2   Alessandra and Toni are going to **make** _____ for the hall.

3   It's a theme party, so we're all going to **wear** _____ .

4   If it rains on Friday, we'll **postpone the** _____ until Saturday.

WILL WE EVER ...?

Many people have questions about the future – will we ever do X or Y, or Z? In this week's magazine, Dr. Sofia Wright answers some of your questions.

📖 READING

1 **Read the magazine article. Match the paragraphs (A–D) with the answers (1–4).**

1 never ☐
2 in about 20 years' time, perhaps ☐
3 only in about a hundred years' time ☐
4 not while Dr. Wright is still living ☐

2 **Read the article again and answer the questions.**

0 What are the two main problems with trying to live on the moon?

There is very little oxygen on the moon and there isn't any animal or plant life.

1 Why does Dr. Wright say "Sorry!" at the end of her answer to question B?

_____

_____

2 What are the two main problems with trying to live under the sea?

_____

_____

3 Why don't people want to take part in experiments instead of animals?

_____

_____

Ⓐ Will people ever live on the moon?
Anouk, Amsterdam

Not in the near future. There are a number of real problems that stop this from happening – the big one is that people need oxygen to stay alive and the moon has very little of it. And what's more, there's no animal or plant life on the moon, so what will we do about getting food? I think one thing is for sure – there won't be anyone there before the next century! And, if it ever happens, I guess the number of people living there will be quite small.

Ⓑ Will we ever be able to travel through time? *Steve, Cambridge*

Well, people have been curious about the idea of time travel for a long time. But that doesn't mean it'll ever be possible. I'd love to be able to go into the past or the future! But I'm sure we'll never be able to. So my answer to this is no, no chance! (Sorry!)

Ⓒ There will never be cities under the sea, will there? *Anthea, Berlin*

You'll be surprised to know that a lot of people are working on this. But, as you can imagine, there are a lot of difficult issues. One is that people need sunlight and there isn't much sunlight 100 meters under the sea! And another is pressure – how can we build walls that are thick enough to keep the water out? And where will the energy we need to power things come from? Personally, I don't think we'll see underwater cities in my lifetime. And to be honest, I'd hate to live under the sea and not see the sun!

Ⓓ Will scientists ever stop using animals for experiments? *Filippo, Bologna*

I hope so. The problem is that people don't like using animals to test new medicines and drugs, but they don't really want to use human beings either. Nobody knows for sure what will happen to the people during the experiments. It's a big risk. What will we do if people become seriously ill or even die during an experiment? However, some people predict that human beings will replace animals more and more in experiments in the next 10 to 20 years. All animal lovers hope they're right. And so do I.

3 **CRITICAL THINKING Read the answers again and underline the facts with a straight line and the writer's opinions with a zig-zag line.**

A

Not in the near future. There are a number of real problems that stop this from happening – the big one is that <u>people need oxygen to stay alive and the moon has very little</u>. And <u>there's no animal or plant life on the moon</u>, so what will we do about food? <u>I think one thing is for sure – it won't be before the next century! And, the number of people living there will be quite small.</u>

An invitation

INVITATION 15

It's party time, everyone! I'm going to be 15 next month! Come to my party and help me celebrate!

Date: Saturday, June 26th
Time: From 8 until late!
Venue: The Mill Room at the Grove Street Youth Club
All you have to bring is yourself (casual dress!)
Love from, Jenna
Reply to **jennahall58@think.mail**

1  **Read the invitation and answer the questions.**

1 What day and time is the party?

_____

2 Where is the party?

_____

3 What do people have to bring?

_____

2 Read the replies to the invitation in Exercise 1 and answer the questions.

1 Who's going to the party?

_____

2 Who isn't going and why not?

_____

A

Jenna
Jennahall58@think.mail

Hi Jenna,

Wow – your birthday! Your party is going to be just great!

Thanks for inviting me, but I'm afraid I can't come. My parents have already booked our vacation and we're leaving the night before your party! Can you believe it?

I'm so sorry, but have a wonderful time, OK? Maybe we can have our own celebration when I'm back from my trip – how about it?

Lots of love, Susanna

3 **Read the phrases.** Circle **Y (saying yes), N (saying no), or T (saying thanks).**

0	I'm afraid I can't come.	Y /(N)/ T
1	Count me in.	Y / N / T
2	Thanks for inviting me.	Y / N / T
3	See you there / then.	Y / N / T
4	I'm so sorry, but …	Y / N / T
5	I'll be there.	Y / N / T
6	I was so happy to get your invitation.	Y / N / T

✏ WRITING TIP: an invitation

- Thank your friend for the invitation.
- Say whether you can go or not.
- Give a reason / add a comment.
- Offer to bring or do something.
- Finish with a friendly phrase.
- Write in a friendly style using informal language.

4 **Now read Tamara's invitation and plan two replies: one to accept and one to refuse. Use the Writing tip to help you.**

★ Tamara
Tamara@thinkmail.com

Hi!

School's out and next Sunday, we're going to have a party to celebrate. It's at seven o'clock at my house. Please let me know if you can come.

Looking forward to seeing you all!

Tamara

5 **Write your two replies, in about 60–80 words each. Use the phrases and functions in Exercise 3 and your plans from Exercise 4 to help you.**

B

Jenna
Jennahall58@think.mail

Hey Jenna,

I was so happy to get your invitation! I can't believe it's your birthday already! I love parties, so count me in. I'll be there. Parties aren't the same without me! My cousin Lennox is staying with me that weekend, so he can come, too! Hope that's OK with you.

Can't wait to see you on the 26th. See you then if not before.

Hugs, Luis

🎧 LISTENING

1 🔊 **7.02** **Listen to the conversation between Scarlett and Enrico about a day out with their friends. Complete the sentences.**

1 The friends are going to _____ .
2 The trip is on _____ .
3 They are going to travel by _____ .

2 🔊 **7.02** **Listen again. Circle the correct answers.**

0 First Scarlett and Enrico talk about
  A how to get there.
  B which day to go.
  C where to meet.

1 How long will it take to ride there?
  A ten hours
  B thirty minutes
  C one and a half hours

2 Enrico's going to take something to
  A play with.
  B listen to.
  C read.

3 What will the friends do for lunch?
  A each take their own picnic
  B share the food they bring
  C buy some food at the store

DIALOGUE

3 🔊 **7.02** **Match the statements with the replies. Then listen again and check.**

0 Hey Enrico, I'm really looking forward to our trip to the beach on Saturday. `d`
1 Right, well, we need to start making some plans, don't we? ☐
2 Well, one thing's certain, we're all going by bike. ☐
3 You know me, I don't want to get up too early on the weekend. ☐
4 I think it's more fun. ☐

a Oh, are we?
b So do I. Great plan!
c Yeah, I guess so.
d Yes! So am I. I can't wait.
e Ha, ha, neither do I.

PHRASES FOR FLUENCY → SB p.72

4 🔊 **7.03** **Put the conversation in the correct order. Then listen and check.**

☐ **Jordan** Lucky you! I think Lucy's a really nice girl.

☐ **Jordan** In other words, you haven't studied for it! Wow! You know, I spent five hours last night studying.

☐ **Jordan** No, I don't think so. There's nothing wrong with studying.

`1` **Jordan** Hey, Joe. Have you heard? There isn't going to be a test tomorrow.

☐ **Jordan** Yes, that's a good plan – she loves movies!

☐ **Joe** So do I. I think we'll go to the movies. What do you think?

☐ **Joe** Five hours? That's a shame. I think you wasted your time.

☐ **Joe** Thank goodness! I was worried about that test because I really wasn't ready for it.

☐ **Joe** Maybe not. Well, look, I have to go. I'm going out with Lucy tonight.

5 **Complete the conversations with the phrases in the list.**

> ~~thank goodness~~ | lucky you | in other words
> What do you think | there's nothing wrong with
> that's a shame

1 **A** I had an accident yesterday. But I wasn't hurt – ___*thank goodness*___ !
  B Well, _____ ! The last time I had an accident, I broke my arm!

2 **A** Thanks for the invitation. But I have another party that night.
  B So, _____ , you can't come? Well, _____ – I really wanted you to be there!

3 **A** I think my hair looks terrible. _____ ?
  B No, it looks fine. _____ it, honestly!

B1 Preliminary for Schools

READING
Part 1: 3-option multiple choice

1 For each question, choose the correct answer.

1

WANTED
DRUMMER FOR ROCK BAND
Must have own drums.
No beginners.
Come to Music Room 5 on Tuesday
after school.

The band would like a musician who

A is free to practise on weekdays.

B has some experience.

C can play the band's drums.

2

About us	News	School life	Timetables

Last week one of our students was nearly knocked down outside the school gates. If you drive your children to school, please leave and collect them in the car park down the road from school.

The school wants parents to

A drive more quickly near the school.

B leave their children in a place that is safe for everyone.

C encourage their children to walk to school.

3

CHESTER ZOO

Children under 12 must be accompanied by an adult at all times.
For school trips:
No more than 15 children per teacher.

A No more than 12 students in a group.

B Adults can only accompany one child each.

C Children can't enter without an adult.

4

THIS SUNDAY'S TRIP TO YORK –
ONE PLACE LEFT

Speak to Miss Higgins to sign up.
Any students going must pay the full fee at reception by Friday at the latest.

A The school trip is now completely full.

B Miss Higgins is accepting money now.

C Some students must give the school some money by the end of the week.

5

WARNING!
DO NOT ENTER!
THIS BUILDING IS PROTECTED BY DOGS AND THERE ARE CCTV CAMERAS EVERYWHERE.

A You can take photos or videos inside the building.

B Please leave animals outside.

C This building has a good security system.

EXAM GUIDE: READING PART 1

In B1 Preliminary for Schools Reading Part 1, you have to read five short texts and choose the option that has the same meaning as the text. The texts can be messages, emails, signs, postcards, notices, labels or websites.

- Think about where you might see each text. What the text looks like might be a clue: a notice in a public place, for example.
- Read each text carefully to get the general meaning.
- Look at each of the options and try to match them to the information in the text.
- Don't choose an option just because it has the same words as the text.
- When you've made your choice, read the text and the options again to check your answer.

Grammar rap!

▶ 23

⊙ GRAMMAR
Simple past vs. past continuous (review) → SB p.76

1 ★☆☆ **Look at the picture. Complete the sentences with the past continuous of the verbs in the list.**

> draw | look | play | read | ~~send~~ | sleep

When the teacher came into the classroom, …

0 Harry _____was sending_____ a text message.

1 Chloe _____ a picture on the board.

2 Jessica and Sophie _____ a magazine.

3 Simon _____ .

4 Sarah _____ out of the window.

5 Milo and Gabriel _____ soccer.

2 ★★☆ (Circle) the correct words.

0 I *did* / (*was doing*) some shopping when I (*met*) / *was meeting* my friend Sadia.

1 When you *got* / *were getting* to the party, everyone *danced* / *was dancing*.

2 It *snowed* / *was snowing*, so my friends *decided* / *were deciding* to stay at home.

3 While the students *walked* / *were walking* in the park, it *started* / *was starting* to rain.

4 I *fell* / *was falling* asleep while we *watched* / *were watching* a movie on TV.

5 Toby *didn't answer* / *wasn't answering* the phone because he *listened* / *was listening* to music with headphones.

3 ★★★ **Complete the text with the correct past tense form of the verbs.**

Izzy and Grace ⁰_____*were sitting*_____ (sit) in a café. They ¹_____ (not look) out of the window – they ²_____ (talk). Just then, the waitress ³_____ (scream) and ⁴_____ (drop) the girls' coffee on the floor. When they ⁵_____ (turn) around, she ⁶_____ (look) out to the street. They ⁷_____ (look) out, too and saw a young man who ⁸_____ (get) out of a big car. The waitress ⁹_____ (run) outside and ¹⁰_____ (go) up to him. She ¹¹_____ (hold) a piece of paper. When the waitress ¹²_____ (come) back into the café, she ¹³_____ (smile). She had her favorite singer's autograph, but Izzy and Grace still didn't have any coffee.

used to → SB p.77

4 ★★☆ **Complete the conversation with the correct form of *used to* and the verbs in the list.**

> buy | eat | have | ~~listen~~ | listen | play | wear | write

Joseph	When you were young, did you have TV?
Grandpa	No, we ⁰_____*used to listen*_____ to the radio.
Joseph	¹_____ with your friends?
Grandpa	Yes, we played soccer, but we didn't have skateboards, just roller skates.
Joseph	What about shopping?
Grandpa	My mother ²_____ food in small stores, not in supermarkets. She always had to cook for us. We ³_____ fast food.
Joseph	What, no burgers?! ⁴_____ to music?
Grandpa	Of course. We had a record player.
Joseph	What was school like?
Grandpa	Well, we ⁵_____ a uniform. And we ⁶_____ everything in our notebooks – no computers then. But we ⁷_____ a lot of fun. Why all these questions?
Joseph	I'm doing a history project.
Grandpa	Ah, OK. I guess I'm part of history now!

Second conditional → SB p.79

5 ★☆☆ **Match the parts of the sentences.**

0 If I knew Hannah's new phone number, `e`
1 If my laptop was working, ☐
2 I would walk to the shopping mall ☐
3 Mom would take me in the car ☐
4 I would buy some new jeans ☐
5 If I went to the shopping mall, ☐

a if it wasn't raining.
b if I asked her nicely.
c I would send her an email.
d I would probably meet some of my friends.
e I would text her.
f if I had more money.

6 ★★☆ **Circle the correct words.**

Adam What ⁰*did /* **would** you do if you ⁰**were** / *would be* alone in a strange city?

Belle I ¹*didn't / wouldn't* go out. If I ²*went / would go* out alone, I ³*was / would be* scared of getting lost.

Adam But what ⁴*did / would* happen if you ⁵*got / would get* lost?

Belle If I ⁶*got / would get* lost, I ⁷*started / would start* to panic.

Adam ⁸*Did / Would* you ask a stranger for help?

Belle No way! I ⁹*called / would call* someone.

Adam I ¹⁰*didn't / wouldn't* be worried if I ¹¹*got / would get* lost. I think I ¹²*will use / would use* the GPS on my phone.

7 ★★★ **Complete the sentences so that they are true for you.**

0 If I met a famous singer, __*I would ask for a selfie.*__
1 If I could visit any place in the world, I _____
2 I would be very happy if _____
3 It would be really bad if _____
4 My home town would be more interesting if _____
5 If I didn't live here, I _____
6 If I didn't have to go to school, I _____
7 The world would be better if _____

I wish → SB p.79

8 ★★☆ **Look at the pictures. Complete the sentences with the correct conditional form and the words in the list.**

astronaut | curly | ~~dance~~ | new | sing | stronger

0 I wish _I could dance._   3 I wish _____

1 I wish _____   4 I wish _____

2 I wish _____   5 I wish _____

GET IT RIGHT!

wish vs. hope

Learners sometimes overuse *I wish* where *I hope* is needed.

✓ I **hope** you will be with me next time.
✗ I ~~wish~~ you will be with me next time.

Complete the sentences with *wish* or *hope*.

0 I ___*wish*___ I could be there, too, but I have to visit my cousin.
1 I _____ you have a good time in Turkey.
2 I _____ I could go there for my birthday.
3 I _____ the weather here was as nice as it is where you are.
4 I _____ things go well for you in your new town.
5 I'm going to get this finished by five – well, I _____ I can, anyway.

73

VOCABULARY
Direction and movement → SB p.76

1 ★☆☆ Look at the picture. Complete the sentences with the words in the list.

around | away from | backward | down
forward | toward | up | up and down

0 There's a snake. It's moving ___around___ a tree.

1 There's a lion. It's going slowly _____ a white rabbit.

2 There's a small white mouse. It's running _____ the tree.

3 There's a large black mouse. It's running _____ the tree.

4 There's a cat. It's running _____ a dog.

5 There's a kangaroo. It's jumping _____ .

6 There's a monkey. It's swinging _____ and _____ on a rope.

2 ★★☆ Complete the sentences with direction and movement phrases.

0 Two boys are playing in the elevator. They've already gone ___up and down___ six times.

1 It's difficult to walk _____ because you can't see where you're going.

2 I was scared when I saw the tiger coming _____ me.

3 I think he was angry with me because he just turned around and walked _____ me, and out of the door.

4 The children were really excited. They were running _____ the room and shouting.

5 It took two hours to get into the exhibition. The line moved _____ very slowly.

Science → SB p.79

3 ★★☆ Use the clues 1–8 to complete the puzzle. What's the mystery word?

0 I'm going to do some ___research___ for my science project at school.

1 Some people hope to _____ a way to build cities under the sea.

2 Did Edison _____ the telephone, or was it someone else?

3 Maybe one day they'll find a _____ for every disease – but perhaps not!

4 Some jobs can't be done by a _____ – they have to be done by people.

5 I think the elevator was a very important _____ . It changed buildings completely.

6 Today we did an _____ with electricity.

7 What do you think is the most important scientific _____ of all time?

8 Our school has a _____ , where we have our science class.

4 ★★☆ Match the parts of the sentences to make a paragraph.

0 My brother loves   [f]
1 He likes to think the kitchen is   [ ]
2 He's done a lot of   [ ]
3 He looks on the internet to   [ ]
4 Sometimes he just   [ ]
5 He'd like to make   [ ]
6 He thinks he's a sort of   [ ]
7 I wish he could find   [ ]

a discover new ways to make sandwiches.
b research into how to make sandwiches.
c a machine for putting butter on bread.
d food scientist, in fact.
e a cure for my stomachache.
f doing experiments in the kitchen.
g his laboratory.
h invents his own.

REFERENCE

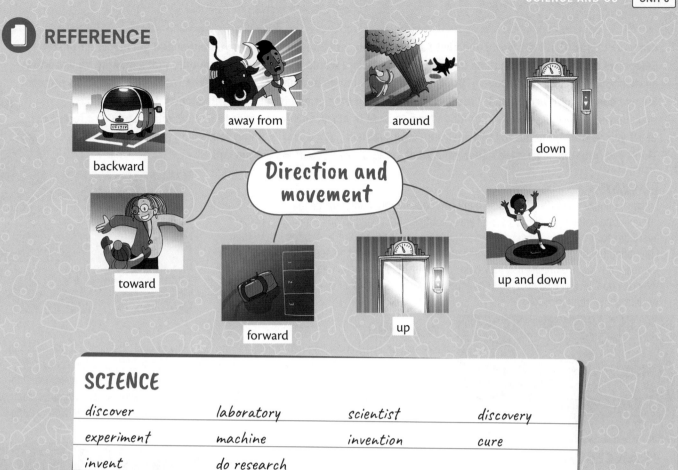

backward | away from | around | down | toward | forward | up | up and down

Direction and movement

SCIENCE

discover	laboratory	scientist	discovery
experiment	machine	invention	cure
invent	do research		

VOCABULARY *EXTRA*

1 Write the words in the list under the pictures.

binoculars | compass | magnifying glass | ~~microscope~~ | periscope | telescope

0 _microscope_   1 _____   2 _____   3 _____   4 _____   5 _____

2 Circle the correct answers.

0 You use these to see things that are far away.
  A magnifying glass   **B** binoculars   **C** compass

1 This makes objects look larger.
  A periscope   **B** compass   **C** magnifying glass

2 This helps you find the right direction. Its needle always points north.
  A compass   **B** binoculars   **C** microscope

3 You use this to examine very small objects.
  A periscope   **B** microscope   **C** telescope

4 You use this to see things that are above water while you are under water.
  A binoculars   **B** telescope   **C** periscope

5 This can help you to see stars and planets at night.
  A telescope   **B** magnifying glass   **C** compass

CITIZEN SCIENCE

Are you curious about the world and about science? You could become a Citizen Scientist and get involved! Citizen Science is scientific research done by ordinary people. You would join a global community that's making an important contribution to scientific discovery. Scientists depend on huge amounts of data for their research, so most CS projects involve collecting information. If Citizen Scientists didn't help, it would take scientists much longer to make discoveries. CS projects cover everything from insects to stars, so you are sure to find something you're interested in. [0]If you're worried about today's environmental problems, it's a way of doing something positive to help. Think you might be interested? Then read what some Citizen Scientists are saying!

EDWARD

I always choose short CS projects so that I can find out about different things. [1]At the moment, I'm counting butterflies, but last year, I was counting birds. I had to go to the same place every day for three days, watch for ten minutes and count the number of birds I saw. Then I identified the birds on a special app and entered the numbers I had seen. Bird and butterfly numbers are important because they help scientists understand the health of the environment. Why do I do CS? I love science and I'm especially interested in nature – I wish I could be a wildlife photographer!

TAMSIN

Last winter, I was collecting information for the Dark Sky project. It's all about observing the increase in light pollution because it has a negative effect on wildlife and the ecosystem. I chose a group of stars on the app and I used to go outside to look at them every evening unless it was cloudy or raining. I had to match them to one of seven maps and enter the time and weather conditions. [2]I'd do another project if I wasn't so busy with schoolwork. I hope I'll be a real scientist one day – maybe an astronomer.

FRANCESCA

[3]When I started the Weather Watch project, they sent me a special plastic tube to collect rainwater. Every morning, I used to write down the amount of rain from the previous 24 hours. When it hadn't rained, I entered 0. Scientists compare this year's rainfall with past years to see how our weather is changing. I chose this project because climate change worries me and it's my way of helping. I also love the idea of taking part in an experiment with thousands of people around the world. Are you interested in science? If I was you, I'd join a CS project – you'd learn something new and you'd help scientific progress!

📖 READING

1 Read the text and answer the questions.

  1 What do the letters CS mean?

  _____

  2 What is Citizen Science?

  _____

  3 Why do scientists need the help of ordinary people?

  _____

  4 Why is it important?

  _____

2 Read the text again. Answer the questions with E (Edward), T (Tamsin), or F (Francesca).

  Which student

  1 took part in a project about the climate? ____

  2 never chooses long projects? ____

  3 would like to work as a scientist? ____

  4 advises other students to become Citizen Scientists? ____

  5 had to watch something at a certain time of day? ____

  6 is curious about the natural world? ____

3 CRITICAL THINKING Look at these sentences from the text and for each one, decide if the information is: A – necessary, giving information about the topic, or B – not essential to understand the topic.

  0 If you're worried about today's environmental problems, it's a way of doing something positive to help. $\boxed{B}$

  1 At the moment, I'm counting butterflies, but last year I was counting birds. $\square$

  2 I'd do another project if I wasn't so busy with schoolwork. $\square$

  3 When I started the Weather Watch project, they sent me a special plastic tube to collect rainwater. $\square$

PRONUNCIATION

The /juː/ sound Go to page 120. 🎧

DEVELOPING Writing

A short text

1 **INPUT** Read the text quickly. Check (✓) the best title.

A The History of Transportation ☐   **B** Cars of the Future ☐   **C** Car Revolution ☐

For thousands of years, people used animals such as horses to get from one place to another. Then, at the beginning of the 20th century, the invention of cars changed the way we moved around forever. It took only a few years for people to make the move from animals to cars, so the move from gasoline-powered cars to driverless electric cars will be even faster. The next transportation revolution has already started!

Traffic creates huge environmental problems, so cities and towns around the world are looking for solutions. Scientists have invented driverless cars that run on electricity instead of gasoline or diesel. Computer scientists have developed software for transportation apps such as ride- and bike-sharing. If we put these inventions together, we could free our cities from traffic.

If there was more progress in transportation technology, we wouldn't need to own cars anymore. Instead we'd call a driverless car when we needed it. It would take us where we wanted to go and we'd get another one to go home. Driverless electric cars can work 24 hours a day, so we also wouldn't need as many parking lots and garages. Electricity is much cleaner than gasoline, so the air would be cleaner, too.

Let's hope the transportation revolution will come to our towns – soon!

2 Read the text again and answer the questions.

According to the text,

1 what was the first transportation revolution? When did it happen?
_____

2 what problems would driverless electric cars solve?
_____

3 **ANALYZE** In the text, find examples of:

1 a second conditional _____
2 a comparison _____
3 a wish for the future _____

4 Match the paragraphs with the time and content.

Paragraph 1   Present   How we'll travel without cars
Paragraph 2   Past   The situation at the moment
Paragraph 3   Future   The last big change in transportation

WRITING TIP: a short text

- Give your text a good title that will attract readers' attention.
- Introduce the topic of the text in the first paragraph.
- Write about the details in the other paragraph(s).
- Write a conclusion.
- Write in an informal style and speak directly to your reader.

5 **PLAN** You are going to write a short text about an invention that you think has changed / will change people's lives. Write a plan using the Writing tip to help you.

Paragraph 1 _____
Paragraph 2 _____
Paragraph 3 _____

6 **PRODUCE** Write a short text in 150–200 words. Use your plan from Exercise 5. Remember to give it an interesting title and write in paragraphs.

🎧 LISTENING

1 🔊 **8.03** **Listen to the two conversations. Match them with the correct picture.**

 A

 C

 B

 D

2 🔊 **8.03** **Listen again and answer the questions.**

Conversation 1

0 Whose vase did the girl's brother break?
He broke Diana's mother's vase.

1 Who did her brother tell about the broken vase?
_____

2 Why would John maybe not do the same thing?
_____

Conversation 2

3 Why is Mimi so happy?
_____

4 Why isn't Michael very enthusiastic?
_____

5 What would happen if someone said, "It wasn't a goal"?
_____

DIALOGUE

3 🔊 **8.04** **Put the conversations in the correct order. Then listen and check.**

Conversation 1

☐ A www.helpyourenglish.net

☐ A I know – but I'm much better now! I used to spend hours studying at home – but then I found a great website.

[1] A Hey, look! I got 79% on the English test.

☐ A Why not?

☐ B Oh, yes – I know that one. I used to use it a lot. But not anymore.

☐ B Because I found a better one. And look – I got 92% on the English test!

☐ B 79%? That's great. But you used to be really bad at English.

☐ B Oh, yes? What's it called?

Conversation 2

☐ A So he doesn't work there anymore?

[1] A I can't go out tonight. I'm working on a presentation about experiments on animals.

☐ A Your dad? Why?

☐ A Your dad worked in a laboratory like that?

☐ B Because he used to work in a laboratory where they tested things on animals.

☐ B No, he left after a year. Now he works in a pet store – he loves it!

☐ B Yes, but he hated it. He used to come home very depressed and we felt really sorry for him.

☐ B Animal testing? Really? You should talk to my dad, then.

Train to TH!NK

Using criteria

4 **Read the text on page 77 again. Then match the parts of the sentences.**

0 Cars replaced animals for transportation because [c]

1 The change to driverless electric cars will be quicker because ☐

2 We need to find a solution to the issue of traffic because ☐

3 Driverless electric cars would be better in cities because ☐

4 Electricity is better than gas because ☐

a all the necessary technology will soon be available.

b it produces less air pollution.

c they were faster and more comfortable.

d it is a huge problem in many cities.

e they are cleaner and more efficient than gas cars.

5 **Imagine private cars are not allowed in cities. Choose the three best ways to get around the city and explain why.**

> bike | bus | driverless cars | e-bike | scooter
> skates | train | tram | subway | walking

1 _____ because _____
2 _____ because _____
3 _____ because _____

B1 Preliminary for Schools

📖 **READING**
Part 5: Multiple-choice cloze

1   For each question, choose the correct answer.

Caroline Herschel, astronomer

Caroline Herschel was born in Germany in 1750. She is ¹_____ to be the first professional female astronomer. She made many important ²_____ that won awards for her work in science.

Caroline wasn't interested in astronomy until after she moved to England to live with her brother William, who was King George III's astronomer. She became William's assistant to write notes about what he ³ _____ in the sky. Caroline often spent long nights looking at stars through her telescope, so she began keeping a ⁴_____ of the comets and new groups of stars that she saw. In 1787, the King of England hired Caroline as an astronomer because he was impressed by her skills. This made her the first woman to ever receive a ⁵_____ as a scientist. After returning to Germany in 1822, she ⁶_____ working as an astronomer until she passed away at the age of 97.

1 **A** respected	**B** accepted	**C** considered	**D** judged
2 **A** discoveries	**B** opportunities	**C** achievements	**D** results
3 **A** realised	**B** checked	**C** searched	**D** noticed
4 **A** record	**B** composition	**C** study	**D** comment
5 **A** value	**B** salary	**C** fare	**D** pay
6 **A** managed	**B** carried	**C** lasted	**D** continued

EXAM GUIDE: READING PART 5

In B1 Preliminary for Schools Reading Part 5, you read a short text with six gaps. You then have to choose the correct word to complete each gap.

- Read the text quickly, ignoring the gaps.
- Read the sentences with the gaps very carefully.
- Make sure you read before and <u>after</u> the gap.
- Look at the options and exclude the ones you know are wrong.
- Try the words in the gap and decide which sounds best.
- Re-read the sentence with the word to check it is right.

CONSOLIDATION

🎧 LISTENING

1 🔊 8.05 **Listen to the conversation. Check (✓) A, B, or C.**

1 What is the weather like as they are talking?

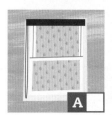 A
 B
 C

2 The boy says that spring is already starting. How does he know?

 A
 B
 C

3 Where does the girl think they could have a party?

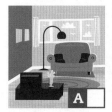 A
 B
 C

2 🔊 8.05 **Listen again. Mark the sentences T (true) or F (false).**

0 It's summer. [F]

1 The boy would like to stop winter from happening. ☐

2 The boy likes to hear birds singing. ☐

3 The boy thinks they could have a party at the end of the month. ☐

4 You can get 20 people in the apartment. ☐

5 The girl's parents have a big yard. ☐

Ⓖ GRAMMAR

3 **Complete the sentences with one word in each space.**

0 I go running every morning, and so ___does___ my friend Monica.

1 I wish you _____ here – but you aren't!

2 When I was younger, I _____ to think there were monsters under my bed!

3 **A** I really don't like cold showers.

  B _____ do I!

4 You can't come? That's a shame. I really wish you _____ .

4 **Correct the sentences.**

0 My sister doesn't like science, and so do I.
  My sister doesn't like science, and neither do I.

1 If I knew the answer, I told you.
  _____

2 He's read this book, isn't he?
  _____

3 I wish my sister is nicer to me.
  _____

4 I wish I can go out tonight, but I have homework.
  _____

🅰🆉 VOCABULARY

5 **Read the clues and complete the crossword.**

Down

0 I think we're going to move later … year.

3 I saw this big dog. It was running … me. I was so scared.

4 I'll come and see you the … after tomorrow.

6 He's a little late, but he'll be here … too long.

8 We're going to … a DJ for the party.

Across

1 It's a … party – we've chosen sports.

2 Alexander Graham Bell … the telephone.

5 I was scared of the dog, so I ran … from it.

7 She's a scientist – she does … into new materials for building.

9 Our party is on the 18th, two weeks from … .

10 I'm writing a … list for the party – I'm inviting a lot of people!

DIALOGUE

6 🔊 **8.06** **Complete the conversation with the phrases in the list. Then listen and check.**

> forgotten about | In other words | lucky you
> around and around | thank goodness | That's a shame
> there's nothing wrong with | What do you think

Hayley   Hi, Eric. Listen, I want to say sorry for yesterday. I didn't mean to get angry. I'm sorry I said those things.

Eric   Oh, that's OK, Hayley. I've
⁰ _____*forgotten about*_____ it already.

Hayley   Really? ¹_____,
you're OK with it?

Eric   Sure. I think we should still be friends.
²_____ ?

Hayley   I think that's awesome. Thanks! And I promise I won't speak to you like that again.

Eric   Well, you know, ³_____
getting angry. I mean, it happens to everyone. But sometimes people say things they don't really mean.

Hayley   Yes, you're right of course. And honestly, I don't get angry like that very often –
⁴_____ !

Eric   Well, ⁵_____ ! I wish I could say the same.

Hayley   Oh? Do you often get angry?

Eric   Yeah, I get angry a lot, and I get these mean thoughts that go ⁶_____
inside my head. Oh, anyway, let's not talk about that. Let's go and get some coffee.

Hayley   I'm sorry, I can't. I have to go home.

Eric   ⁷_____ . But OK,
another day. See you tomorrow, Hayley.

 ## READING

7 **Read the article. Match the missing phrases with the correct places (A–E).**

0 and meet to speak it   D

1 when *Star Trek* included them   ☐

2 in the 1960s and 1970s   ☐

3 the deepest parts of outer space   ☐

4 played by William Shatner   ☐

One of the greatest successes in science fiction is the TV series *Star Trek*.

The series features the *Starship Enterprise*, which has gone out into space on a mission to explore **[A]** and to make contact with other civilizations. When it started in 1966, it was probably the best science fiction anywhere on TV or in movies. The series was remarkable because members of the crew of the Enterprise included women and people of different races, something that TV **[B]** didn't show very often.

A few years later, a second series called *Star Trek: The Next Generation* appeared, with Patrick Stewart as Jean-Luc Picard, the captain of the Enterprise – quite a different figure from the original Captain Kirk, **[C]**.

Star Trek is over 50 years old, but it still has a lot of fans. There are "Trekkie" conventions in many places around the world every year. Among the Enterprise's enemies were the Klingons from the planet Klingon and a whole Klingon language has been developed. People learn it **[D]**. There are references to the show in many books, plays, and other TV shows. And it's also interesting to observe that some things that were fiction **[E]** are not fiction any more. Cell phones and sliding doors, for example, seemed incredible in the early episodes, but now they are part of our everyday lives.

✏ WRITING

8 **Write a short text (about 120–150 words) about a science fiction book, movie, or TV show that you really like or really dislike. Include the following information:**

- what the book / movie / TV show is called
- what it is about
- what you like / dislike about it

9 WORKING WEEK

GRAMMAR

The passive: simple present and simple past → SB p.86

1 ★☆☆ Mark the sentences A (present active), B (present passive), C (past active), or D (past passive).

0 Our house wasn't built very well. | D |

1 The recycling bins are emptied every Monday. | |

2 We were late for school again yesterday. | |

3 They're Canadian. | |

4 Dad wasn't in a good mood this morning. | |

5 The weather's horrible today. | |

6 We were defeated in the final by Sid and Fred. | |

7 She's protected by a police officer at all times. | |

2 ★★☆ Complete the conversation with the words in the list.

> are called | aren't called | ask | asked
> offered | was asked | was called
> was offered | wasn't asked | ~~were asked~~
> were you asked | were called

Dean How was the job interview, Dora?

Dora It was OK. There were ten of us. We
⁰ _were asked_ to wait and then we
¹_____ into the interview room
one by one.

Dean What kind of questions ²_____ ?

Dora First, I ³_____ the usual kind, but then
they ⁴_____ really strange ones.

Dean Like what?

Dora OK, here's one: "You ⁵_____ Tom.
How is your life different?"

Dean But you ⁶_____ Tom. You're a girl!

Dora I guess it's a way to see how creative I am.

Dean Did they ⁷_____ you why you want
the job?

Dora No, I ⁸_____ that one.

Dean Oh. So what happened after the interview?

Dora Well, after an hour I ⁹_____ back into
the room. And I ¹⁰_____ the job!

Dean What?!

Dora They ¹¹_____ me the job. I got it!

3 ★★★ Complete the second sentence so that it means the same as the first. Use no more than three words.

0 Someone found my wallet outside the school.
My _wallet was found_ outside the school.

1 They make cars in that factory.
Cars _____ in that factory.

2 They don't charge you to use the computers.
You _____ charged to use
the computers.

3 Nobody saw them leave.
They _____ when they left.

4 People lose a lot of umbrellas on city buses.
A lot of umbrellas _____ on
city buses.

5 An American bought the painting.
The painting _____ an American.

6 They don't cook the meals at the school.
The meals _____ at the school.

7 A famous architect designed the houses.
The houses _____ a famous architect.

4 ★★★ Complete the text with the correct active or passive form of the verbs.

Did you know that millions of letters and packages
⁰ _are delivered_ every day in the US?
But how does a letter get from A to B?
Of course, first it ¹_____ (write) and
then it ²_____ (put) in an envelope.
Then stamps ³_____ (stick) on it and
it ⁴_____ (mail) in a mailbox. A post
office worker ⁵_____ (collect) it and
⁶_____ (take) it to a sorting office. Here,
the letters ⁷_____ (sort) by their zip
codes. This ⁸_____ (do) by a machine,
but in the past it ⁹_____
(not do) by machine – the addresses
¹⁰_____ (read) by people and put
into boxes for various destinations by hand.
Finally, the letters ¹¹_____ (take) by road,
rail, and air to their destination, where postal workers
¹²_____ (give) the letters to deliver.

The passive: present continuous and present perfect
→ SB p.89

5 ⭐☆☆ **Complete the sentences with *been* or *being*.**

0 The new supermarket is ____*being*____ opened.
1 We are _____ followed by that cat!
2 The paintings have _____ stolen.
3 The baby has _____ fed and he's asleep now.
4 The criminals are _____ arrested.
5 The trees are _____ cut down.
6 The door has _____ painted.
7 The windows have _____ broken.

6 ⭐☆☆ Circle the correct words.

0 You can't buy her new book because it *isn't being* / *hasn't been* published yet.
1 The new library isn't open yet – it *is still being* / *has still been* built.
2 This food is horrible – it *isn't being* / *hasn't been* cooked properly.
3 Dinner isn't ready yet – it's *being* / *been* cooked.
4 Look at this red spot on my arm. *I'm being* / *I've been* bitten by a mosquito.
5 He's in an ambulance now. He's *being* / *been* taken to the hospital.
6 There's no cake left – it's all *being* / *been* eaten!
7 I don't have my laptop right now – the screen's *being* / *been* fixed.

7 ⭐⭐⭐ **Rewrite the active sentences in the passive form and the passive sentences in the active form.**

0 Someone took a photo of the president going for a run.
A photo of the president going for a run has been taken.
1 The police are questioning him.
He _____
2 The baby is being given a bath by Willow.
Willow _____
3 A new café has been opened near my house.
They _____
4 They've just made a new James Bond movie.
A new James Bond movie _____
5 A professional chef is cooking the meal.
The meal _____
6 The house is being rented by students.
Students _____
7 They've drunk all the fruit juice.
All the fruit juice _____

8 ⭐⭐☆ **Complete the email with the present perfect passive or present continuous passive of the verbs.**

> **Marianna**
> Marianna@thinkmail.com
>
> Dear Marianna,
>
> The work on our new house is going well and the money ⁰____*hasn't run out*____ (not run out) yet! I'm sending you a photo. As you can see, a lot ¹_____ (do) since you were here in September. The walls ²_____ (build) and the roof ³_____ (put) on. The doors and the windows ⁴_____ (not put) in yet – next week, hopefully. At the moment, most of the work ⁵_____ (do) inside the house. As I'm writing, the walls ⁶_____ (paint) and the kitchen ⁷_____ (install). The bathroom ⁸_____ already _____ (finish). Three more weeks and our new house will be ready! You'll have to come and see it.
>
> Love, Logan

GET IT RIGHT!

Simple present passive vs. present perfect passive

Learners often use the simple present passive where the present perfect passive is required.

✓ I **have been given** a new phone for my birthday.
✗ I *am given* a new phone for my birthday.

Complete the sentences with the correct form of the verbs.

0 I am sorry to inform you that the concert __*has been canceled*__ (cancel).
1 We've been raising money for charity and so far we _____ (give) $150!
2 All the best smartphones _____ (make) in Asia.
3 Nowadays, this type of shark _____ (find) only in North America.
4 I need help – my laptop _____ (attack) by a virus.
5 My bike _____ (steal)! How am I going to get home?
6 In the UK, potato chips _____ (call) crisps.

VOCABULARY
Jobs

1 ★★☆ **Complete the text with the words in the list.**

> career | challenging | earn | ~~long~~ | notice
> on-the-job | paid | pay | promoted | successful

My job is the worst job in the world. I work really
⁰ ___long___ hours – 8 a.m. to 8 p.m. every day.
The ¹_____ is terrible and I just barely
² _____ enough money to live on. I don't get
³ _____ time off and I lose money if I need to
take time off.

When I started, they promised me ⁴_____
training. Well, they showed me how to make a cup of
coffee and that was it! I've been here ten years and I still
haven't been ⁵_____ . I'm doing the same job
I did when I started. And it isn't really the most
⁶ _____ job. I mean, I think I could probably
do it in my sleep.

On my first day here, I was so excited. I really thought
this was the start of my ⁷_____ . I thought
I'd soon be a ⁸ _____ businessman earning
a lot of money. Well, I was wrong. I know what
you're thinking. Why don't I hand in my
⁹_____ ? I can't – the boss is my dad!

work as / in / for

2 ★★☆ **Complete the sentences with the words in the list.**

> fashion | IT | modeling agency | models
> online gaming company | ~~tour guide~~
> tourism | software engineer | travel agency

Elliot works as a ⁰ ___tour guide___ .
He works in ¹_____ .
He works for a small ²_____ .
Annie works for an ³_____ .
She works as a ⁴_____ .
She works in ⁵_____ .
Leon and Elsa work in ⁶_____ .
They work as ⁷_____ .
They work for a ⁸_____ .

3 ★★☆ **Write about a person you know.**

1 My _____ works as _____ .
2 He/She works in _____ .
3 He/She works for _____ .

work vs. job

4 ★☆☆ **Circle the correct words.**

0 I have a great *job* / *work*. I love it.
1 I had a lot of *job* / *work* to do and I didn't get
to bed until 1 a.m.
2 A lot of people lost their *jobs* / *works* when the
factory was closed.
3 She starts her new *job* / *work* next week.
4 I like what I do, but it's very hard *job* / *work* at times.
5 We need to create more *jobs* / *works* in this country.
6 The teacher was really happy with my *job* / *work*.
7 Do you take *job* / *work* home with you sometimes?

WordWise: Time expressions with *in*

5 ★★☆ **Match the parts of the sentences.**

0 What did you decide to do — *f*
1 We hope to get married — ☐
2 People did things differently — ☐
3 How many hot dogs can you eat — ☐
4 He ran 100 meters — ☐
5 The FIFA World Cup is usually — ☐
6 We often go skiing — ☐
7 I can't believe the summer break starts — ☐

a in the past.
b in two weeks' time.
c in the next few years.
d in the winter.
e in under ten seconds.
f in the end?
g in June and July.
h in five minutes?

6 ★★★ **Write a sentence about each of these things.**

1 Something you did in the past (but you don't
do now).
_____

2 Something you're going to do in ten minutes'
time.
_____

3 Something you want to do in the next few years.
_____

4 Something you always do in the summer.
_____

5 Something you can do in less than ten seconds.
_____

6 Something that always happens in December.
_____

REFERENCE

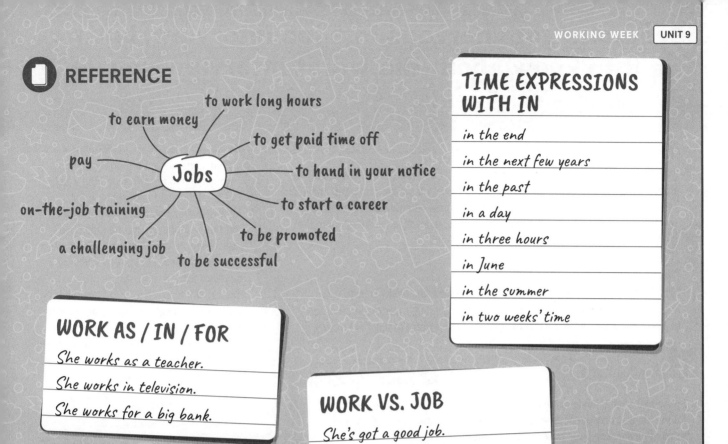

TIME EXPRESSIONS WITH IN

in the end
in the next few years
in the past
in a day
in three hours
in June
in the summer
in two weeks' time

Jobs mind map: to work long hours, to earn money, pay, to get paid time off, to hand in your notice, on-the-job training, to start a career, a challenging job, to be promoted, to be successful

WORK AS / IN / FOR

She works as a teacher.
She works in television.
She works for a big bank.

WORK VS. JOB

She's got a good job.
It's difficult work, but I like it.

VOCABULARY *EXTRA*

1 Check (✓) the correct column.

	At work / In a job	Not working
0 Apply for a job		✓
1 Be in charge		
2 Be out of work		
3 Lose your job		
4 Take time off		
5 Work part-time		

2 Rewrite the sentences with the verb phrases and collocations in Exercise 1.

0 Milly only works in the mornings.
She __works part-time__ .

1 Thomas is responsible for customer service.
He's _____ customer service.

2 It's a good job, so I'll ask if I can have it.
I'm going to _____ the job.

3 Francis was always late for work, so they sent him away.
Francis _____ for being late.

4 Erin hasn't worked for six months.
Erin has been _____ for six months.

5 Laura isn't at work this week. She's on vacation.
Laura has _____ work this week.

Everyone gets nervous in a job interview, but we want to know about the worst interview you've ever had – or given!

I had a job interview for a company in New York. At that time, I lived about 200 km from New York, but I really wanted this job, so I took a three-hour train trip and spent over $100 on tickets. The train arrived late, so I spent another $20 on a taxi to the offices of the company. I got there just in time and was taken straight into the interview. The interviewer asked me his first question.

"Do you speak French?"

"No, I don't," I told him.

"Oh, I'm sorry," he replied. "We really need someone who speaks French."

He stood up, shook my hand, and thanked me for coming. I was really annoyed because this wasn't mentioned in the job ad. What a waste of time and money.

CLAUDIA

I once had a job interview with a law firm. More than 300 people applied for the job and only ten of us were invited for an interview. The interview was exhausting because I was asked a lot of really difficult questions.

However, I was pleased with my answers and I was pretty sure that the interview was going well. I was right. At the end, the interviewer offered me the job and stood up to shake my hand. I stood up, too, but my leg was asleep from sitting down for so long. As soon as I stood up, I fell down backward. Unfortunately, I was shaking the interviewer's hand and I forgot to let go. As I fell, I pulled him down with me onto the floor. It was very embarrassing. Amazingly, I still got the job.

NATHAN

I once interviewed a man for a job. He came into my office wearing a pair of headphones. I invited him to sit down, thinking he was going to take off the headphones, but he didn't. So I asked him, "Would you mind taking off the headphones? It might be easier to interview you."

"Oh, it's OK," he replied. "I can hear you OK and I find listening to music helps me relax." He wasn't offered the job. Neither was the man who brought his rabbit into the interview room and asked me if I could get him some water for the rabbit to drink!

REBECCA

📖 READING

1 Read the magazine article. How is Rebecca different from Claudia and Nathan?

2 Read the article again. Mark the sentences T (true), F (false), or DS (the text doesn't say).

0 Claudia spent over $100 to get to her interview. `T`

1 Claudia got the money back for her train and taxi. ☐

2 Nathan had to compete with over 300 people to get the job. ☐

3 Nathan wasn't confident in his interview. ☐

4 The interviewer wasn't happy when Nathan pulled him onto the floor. ☐

5 Nathan still works at the law firm. ☐

6 The man wore headphones because he had a hearing problem. ☐

7 Rebecca gave one of the men a job. ☐

3 Which of these stories do you think is the funniest? Why?

_____

_____

_____

4 `CRITICAL THINKING` Who was responsible for the disasters in each interview? Circle the correct answers, and then match them to a reason (A–C).

1 *Claudia / The interviewer / Both*
Reason: ☐

2 *Nathan / The interviewer / Both*
Reason: ☐

3 *The man with headphones / The interviewer / Both*
Reason: ☐

4 *The man with the rabbit / The interviewer / Both*
Reason: ☐

Reasons:

A His / Her behavior wasn't suitable for an interview. (x2)

B The candidate wasn't given the correct information.

C It was an unlucky accident.

DEVELOPING ✎ *Writing*

Describing a process

1 **INPUT** Read the article quickly. Match texts A and B with the photos.

Print or Digital: how is a book made?

You've written the next bestselling book, so now what? How do you get it published? This week, we look at two different publishing processes...

1

2

Text A
First, the content is written by an author. The author contacts a publisher, directly or through a literary agent.
If the publisher wants to print the book, they ask the author to sign a contract. Then, a team of editors edit the content. At the same time, the cover is designed.
When the book is ready to be printed, it is sent to a printing company (or "printer"). Hundreds or thousands of copies are printed on paper and the books are stored in a big building.
Finally, the book is sent out to bookstores and people can buy it.

Text B
First, the book is written by the author, who uses a special online program that puts the content into an electronic format.
It is then edited by someone the author contacts. The author designs, or asks an artist to design, the digital front cover.
The author chooses where to publish it online and uploads it after signing a contract. At the same time, the digital front cover is uploaded.
Finally, the book is sold online and can be bought and downloaded by people to read on their e-readers, tablets, or cell phones.

2 Read the article again. Circle and complete the sentence with your own idea.

I find the process described in *Text A / Text B* more interesting because _____
_____
_____

3 **ANALYZE** Circle the correct words.

1 *Text A / Text B* focuses on a digital process.
2 Text A requires *more people / fewer people* to be part of the process than Text B.
3 *Text A / Text B* is about doing something by yourself.
4 Many verbs are in the passive in *Text A / both texts*.

4 Write the passive verbs used in each stage for Text A in the active.

Stage 1: _____
Stage 2: _____
Stage 3: _____
_____
Stage 4: _____

✎ WRITING TIP: describing a process

- Identify the stages of the process.
- Find the verbs you need to use for each stage.
- Use the passive form of verbs where possible.
- Write one paragraph for each stage.
- Write in a formal style.

5 **PLAN** You are going to describe a process. Do some research to find out about a process you are interested in and write some notes. Write a plan, using the Writing tip and texts A and B to help you.

- Think of a process that you know well or research one.
- Identify four or five different stages in the process and put them in chronological order.
- Remember to use the passive when it is needed.
- Link your short paragraphs together using staging words: *first, then, after that, next, when, finally*.

6 **PRODUCE** Write a description of a process in about 130 words. Use your plan from Exercise 5 to help you.

🎧 LISTENING

1 🔊 **9.01** **Listen to the three conversations. Put the activities in the order you hear them.**

- ☐ **A** selling books
- ☐ **B** dancing
- ☐ **C** walking

2 🔊 **9.01** **Listen again and answer the questions.**

0 What are they all raising money for?
To help the people in Cuba after the hurricane.

1 How far is the sponsored walk?
_____

2 When and where is the book sale?
_____

3 What's Caleb going to do on Friday afternoon?
_____

4 Why doesn't Caleb want to do the sponsored dance?
_____

DIALOGUE

3 **Put the words in order to make phrases.**

0 us / join / want / do / you / to
Do you want to join us?

1 in / me / count
_____

2 going / there / to / you / are / be / ?
_____

3 but / love / can't / I'd / to / I
_____

4 you / in / are / so / ?
_____

5 not / sorry / time / no / this
_____

4 **Choose two of the phrases from Exercise 3 and use them to write a four-line conversation.**

A Hi, Beth. Where are you going?

B *I'm going to meet Elena in town. We're going to have lunch. Do you want to join us?*

A I'd love to, but I can't. I have to help my mom.

B Never mind. Maybe next time.

_____
_____
_____
_____

PHRASES FOR FLUENCY → SB p.90

5 🔊 **9.02** **Put the conversation in the correct order. Then listen and check.**

- ☐ **Mason** No, I haven't. I didn't make the mess. Liam did.
- ☐ **Mason** I have to do some research for my history project.
- ☐ **Mason** Mom! Surely you don't think I'd do that!
- ☐ **Mason** Sounds fair. Thanks, Mom.
- ☑ 1 **Mason** Mom, can I use your laptop for a while?
- ☐ **Mom** No – you'd never do that. By the way, have you cleaned your room yet?
- ☐ **Mom** What do you want it for?
- ☐ **Mom** That's not the point. I asked you to do it. Clean the room and then you can use the laptop.
- ☐ **Mom** OK, as long as it *is* for that and not for playing games!

6 **Complete the conversations with the phrases in the list.**

> as long as | by the way | for a while
> sounds | ~~surely~~ | that's not the point

Conversation 1

A Can you help me with my homework?

B Sorry, I'm busy.

A ⁰____*Surely*____ you have ten minutes free.

B Well, ¹_____. Anyway, it's your homework. You should do it on your own.

A OK, if that's how you feel. Oh, ²_____ , don't ask me if you can borrow my bike this weekend. Because you can't.

Conversation 2

A We haven't gone bowling ³_____ . Can we go this weekend?

B ⁴_____ great. ⁵_____ we don't have to invite my sister, too.

A Why not?

B I just don't want her to come.

PRONUNCIATION
/tʃ/ and /dʒ/ consonant sounds Go to page 120.

B1 Preliminary for Schools

🎧 LISTENING
Part 4: 3-option multiple choice

1 🔊 **9.05** **You will hear an interview with a young chef, Abigail. For each question, choose the correct answer.**

1 How was Abigail different to the other competitors in the Young Chef competition?
  A She was very good at cooking.
  B She wasn't at all anxious.
  C She didn't make friends easily.

2 When did Abigail start cooking?
  A when she worked in her friend's parents' restaurant
  B when she did a cooking course as a young teenager
  C when she was very small

3 What does she say about her job in the restaurant?
  A She thinks it's a good learning opportunity for her.
  B She is always given the best jobs to do.
  C She doesn't enjoy it because it's hard work.

4 In her cooking videos,
  A she explains her recipes in great detail.
  B she shows teenagers how to make quick meals.
  C she tells young people to try out new ideas.

5 How does Abigail prefer spending her free time?
  A She likes to try new dishes at local restaurants.
  B She works on new recipes in the kitchen.
  C She cooks her friends' favourite meals for them.

6 Abigail is planning to prepare for her career by
  A cooking new dishes for her parents and family.
  B learning from other chefs.
  C doing a cookery course in France.

EXAM GUIDE: LISTENING PART 4

In B1 Preliminary for Schools Listening Part 4, you will listen to an interview. While you are listening, you have to answer six multiple choice questions.

- Before you listen, read the questions and options to get an idea of what you are going to hear.
- Remember the questions follow the order of the interview.
- You won't hear exactly the same words in the audio as in the questions, so listen for synonyms and phrases with the same meaning.
- During the first listening, start choosing your answers.
- In the second listening, check and correct your answers.

Grammar rap!

▶ 29

GRAMMAR
Past perfect

→ SB p.94

1 ★☆☆ **Match the pictures with the sentences.**

0 When Evie got home, her dad had cooked the dinner. `C`

1 When Evie got home, her dad cooked the dinner. ☐

2 When our friends arrived at the movie theater, the movie started. ☐

3 When our friends arrived at the movie theater, the movie had started. ☐

2 ★☆☆ **Match the parts of the sentences.**

0 I recognized her face, `f`
1 They got to the movie theater ☐
2 As soon as he closed the door, ☐
3 My laptop didn't turn on ☐
4 I didn't think I'd said anything funny, ☐
5 When the exam finished, ☐

a but he couldn't stop laughing.
b because I'd forgotten to charge it.
c I hadn't answered all the questions.
d he knew he'd left his key inside.
e ten minutes after the movie had started.
f but I couldn't remember where I'd met her.

3 ★★☆ **Complete the sentences. Use the past perfect of the verbs in the list.**

do | have | not do | not see
not clean | see | clean

0 I didn't watch the movie because I *'d seen* it before.

1 Alicia didn't invite Patrick to the party because they _____ an argument the day before.

2 Claire's dad was angry with her because she _____ her bedroom.

3 I didn't have to clean the rabbit's cage because Joey _____ already _____ it.

4 The house was looking really nice because Mom and Dad _____ everything.

5 Kim had to miss her break time because she _____ her homework.

6 The driver almost caused an accident because he _____ the red light.

4 ★★★ **Complete the text with either the simple past or the past perfect of the verbs.**

Talia ⁰ *had eaten* (eat) one cookie and was starting on her second when she ¹_____ (start) making strange noises. I ²_____ (look) at her and I ³_____ (know) immediately that a large piece of her cookie ⁴_____ (get) stuck in her throat. Then I ⁵_____ (remember) that years ago I ⁶_____ (attend) a first aid course and that they ⁷_____ (teach) us how to help someone in this situation. I ⁸_____ (run) around Talia, ⁹_____ (put) my arms around her waist, ¹⁰_____ (join) my hands together in front of her, and ¹¹_____ (pull) as hard as I could. Then I ¹²_____ (hear) a little cry from Talia and I ¹³_____ (knew) that the food ¹⁴_____ (come) out. Talia ¹⁵_____ (give) me a big hug. That first aid lesson ¹⁶_____ (probably save) her life.

Past perfect continuous SB p.97

5 ★☆☆ **Put the words in order to make sentences.**

0 been / hours / talking / we / for / had
We had been talking for hours.

1 been / to / they / me / hadn't / listening
_____

2 waiting / long / you / how / had / been?
_____

3 crying / had / morning / she / been / all
_____

4 well / I / been / hadn't / very / feeling
_____

5 had / been / how / it / raining / long?
_____

Past perfect vs. past perfect continuous SB p.97

6 ★☆☆ Circle **the correct words.**

0 I was disappointed. I *had saved /* had been saving all year and I still didn't have enough money.

1 Dad *had cooked / had been cooking* all morning and the kitchen smelled great.

2 They *hadn't eaten / hadn't been eating* anything all day and they were really hungry.

3 Kit *had watched / had been watching* the movie five times, but he still didn't really understand it.

4 We *had walked / had been walking* 30 km before we saw anyone.

5 Adriana failed the test because she *hadn't written / hadn't been writing* enough.

7 ★★☆ **Complete the text with the words in the list.**

~~had been having~~ | hadn't called | hadn't listened
had been snowing | had been waiting
hadn't been sleeping | had written

I **0** *had been having* headaches for a week and I **1**_____ well, so my dad made an appointment for me to see the doctor. We took a taxi to the doctor's because it **2**_____ all morning.

We arrived at 3 p.m. and sat down. We
3_____ for an hour and they still
4_____ me when Dad went to talk to the receptionist. My appointment was for 2 p.m.! Dad **5**_____ properly on the phone and he **6**_____ down the wrong time!

8 ★★★ **Complete the sentences with the verbs. Use one past perfect form and one past perfect continuous form in each pair.**

0 (spend)

A She didn't have any money left because she _____*had spent*_____ it all on a new dress.

B They ___*had been spending*___ too much money for years and now they had none left.

1 (play)

A He _____ only _____ basketball for five minutes when he broke his leg.

B The children _____ all the games in the house and now they were bored.

2 (drink)

A Jacob _____ four glasses of water and now he really needed to use the bathroom.

B He _____ the cup of coffee for more than an hour and now it was cold.

3 (not look)

A Catrina _____ where she was going and that's why she crashed.

B She _____ at her schedule and that's why she missed her appointment.

GET IT *RIGHT!*

Past perfect continuous vs. past continuous

Learners sometimes use the past continuous when the past perfect continuous is required.

✓ We **had been training** for weeks, but we lost.

✗ We ~~were training~~ for weeks, but we lost.

Complete the sentences with the correct form of the verbs.

0 I found his phone under the chair where he _____*had been sitting*_____ (sit).

1 We met by accident when she _____ (walk) her dog.

2 When I saw him, he _____ (carry) a backpack.

3 I _____ (wait) for hours, so I was very happy when he called.

4 I _____ (work) all day, so I decided to go out.

5 He _____ (talk) on his phone when the fire alarm went off.

ᴬᶻ VOCABULARY
Time linkers

`→ SB p.94`

1 ★☆☆ **Complete the sentences with the words in the list.**

> as soon as | then | until | ~~when~~ | while

0 _____When_____ I'm 18, I'm going to go to college.

1 _____ I'm old enough, I'm going to learn to drive.

2 I'm going to meet the right person and _____ I'm going to get married.

3 I'm not going to have children _____ I'm 30.

4 I'm going to find a job at a restaurant _____ I'm in college.

2 ★★★ **Complete the sentences so that they are true for you.**

0 When I'm 18, I'm going to _get a job._

1 As soon as I have enough money, I'm going to _____

2 I'm going to finish school and then _____

3 I'll probably live with my parents until _____

4 I'm going to _____ while I _____

Illness: collocations

`→ SB p.97`

3 ★★☆ **Find five more verbs and five nouns or adjectives to make illness collocations.**

H	A	V	E	A	S	B	D	D	I	N
P	O	H	I	J	V	I	O	W	E	O
Q	A	E	U	B	M	E	C	X	Y	I
D	B	X	I	M	M	W	T	K	S	T
T	N	E	M	T	N	I	O	P	P	A
A	S	R	T	X	C	S	R	B	F	R
K	G	C	L	T	K	T	H	L	F	E
E	J	I	H	J	E	G	S	E	E	P
C	F	S	L	G	L	R	C	R	E	O
K	L	E	K	A	M	J	C	H	L	R

0 _FEEL SICK_

1 _____

2 _____

3 _____

4 _____

5 _____

4 ★★☆ **Put the letters in order to make collocations.**

0 ese a rctood _____see a doctor_____

1 leef ciks _____

2 amek na mpitntpoean _____

3 vaeh na oiranpteo _____

4 teg teertb _____

5 egt meso scexiere _____

5 ★★☆ **Complete the conversations.**

1 A My dad's got to h_____ an o_____ on Monday.

B Oh. I hope it goes well and he g_____ b_____ soon.

2 A Did you s_____ the d_____ yesterday?

B Yes, I did. He told me to g_____ more e_____ .

3 A I'm f_____ really s_____ .

B You'd better m_____ an a_____ with the doctor.

6 ★★☆ **Complete the text with the collocations in Exercise 4. Use the correct form of the verbs.**

I was ⁰_____feeling sick_____ one day a few months ago. I didn't think much about it, but the next day I was still feeling sick and I was also feeling very tired. It was the same the next day and the day after that. My wife told me I should ¹_____ .

Now, I don't really like going to the doctor, but I was starting to get a bit worried. Something just didn't feel right. So I called the doctor that afternoon to ²_____ for the next day.

The doctor did a few tests and he seemed really worried. In fact, he was so worried that he called immediately for an ambulance. I was rushed to the hospital, where they did more tests. Finally, after about five hours, a doctor came and saw me. He said I could have a heart attack at any moment and that I needed to ³_____ immediately.

It was a real shock, but what could I say? So I followed the doctor's orders and spent the next few months ⁴_____ . I went for a check-up the other day and the doctor says I'm fine. I just need to eat a little less and ⁵_____ .

REFERENCE

as soon as

when — Time linkers — then

while   until

ILLNESS: COLLOCATIONS

get exercise

get better

see a doctor

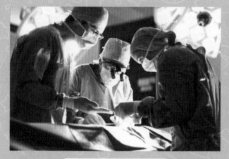
have an operation

make an appointment

feel sick

VOCABULARY *EXTRA*

1 Complete the table with the words in the list.

fit | a heart attack | in the hospital | a prescription | a fever | ~~weight~~

lose	get	stay	have
0 _weight_	1 _____	3 _____	4 _____
	2 _____		5 _____

2 Complete the texts with the words in Exercise 1.

A Last week, Freya felt sick and she had a high ⁰___*fever*___ . She went to the doctor and got a ¹_____ for some medicine. She feels better now.

B Mr. Lewis had a ²_____ . He was taken to the hospital in an ambulance. He had to ³_____ in the hospital for a week because he needed to have an operation. He's back at home now, but he has to ⁴_____ some weight and start doing some exercise to get ⁵_____ .

DR. GOODLIFE talks about ... sleep

A good night's sleep is essential for good health. It's one of the best things we can do to improve our general well-being. If we don't get enough sleep, our minds as well as our bodies suffer, because we need sleep to reset our brain and body. Although we relax while we're asleep, there's a lot of work going on at the same time. It's the time when our body repairs itself and recovers from damage or illness. The mind organizes the day's memories and prepares itself mentally for the next day. Did you know teenagers need 9–9.5 hours of sleep a night? So, are you getting enough of it? To find out how to get a better night's sleep, read these replies to the most frequent comments I hear about sleep!

1 D
You need to turn off all screens at least a half an hour before going to bed. It's difficult to fall asleep as soon as you stop playing games or watching movies because your brain is still very active and processing information.

2 ☐
It's best not to keep any digital equipment in your bedroom at night. Lights and sounds from them can interrupt your sleep and wake you up. A sleep-friendly bedroom is dark, quiet, comfortable, and not too cold or warm.

3 ☐
I'm not surprised! Researchers found that if people had done some exercise during the day, they slept better at night. Try to do some sports or exercise every day because this helps to relax your body.

4 ☐
Coffee and energy drinks keep you from falling asleep and keep you awake because they contain caffeine. It's best to avoid them in the evenings and not to drink too many during the day either!

5 ☐
Going to bed earlier and having a bedtime routine are good for you. Studies found that if people had been doing the same things at the same time and in the same order before going to bed, their bodies relaxed and they fell asleep more easily.

6 ☐
Increasing your sleep time like this doesn't work, I'm afraid, and it can even make you feel worse! Having a regular bedtime every day of the week is important for general sleep health.

7 ☐
If you're anxious, try talking to someone – a parent, sibling, or friend – about your problems. You'll feel calmer afterwards, so you'll be able to sleep better.

📖 READING

1 Read the text. Match the comments (A–G) with the replies (1–7).

  A "Last week, I was training for a basketball game every day and I was sleeping really well."

  B "I'd been worrying about something all day and I didn't close my eyes all night."

  C "I don't like going to bed before 10 p.m."

  D "I went to bed as soon as the movie had finished, but I couldn't sleep."

  E "I'd had one energy drink after swimming and I was awake nearly all night!"

  F "Notifications from my phone often wake me during the night."

  G "When I hadn't slept much during the week, I slept until lunchtime on weekends."

2 Read the text again. Correct the false information in these sentences.

  0 Only our bodies need sleep to stay healthy.
  Our bodies and minds need sleep to stay healthy.

  1 It's a good idea to relax before bed by playing video games.
  _____

  2 You should always sleep with your phone near your bed.
  _____

  3 Some drinks help you sleep well.
  _____

  4 It doesn't matter what time you go to bed.
  _____

  5 If you stay up late, you should sleep longer the next morning.
  _____

3 CRITICAL THINKING Read the text again. Complete the table with short notes.

For a good night's sleep,	
you should	you shouldn't
✓ _____	✗ _____
✓ _____	✗ _____
✓ _____	✗ _____

DEVELOPING Writing

A story

1 **INPUT** Read the story quickly and find two mistakes in the picture.

_____
_____

Home   About   Blog   Archives

POSTED: TODAY

It was a cold and windy day and it was raining hard, but we'd decided to play the game anyway. We'd been playing for over an hour and the score was 0–0. I'd just missed scoring a goal when I slipped on the wet grass and fell down. I knew something was wrong when I felt the pain in my ankle. I tried to stand up but couldn't. While I was lying on the ground, holding my ankle, I heard a cheer. My team had scored a goal, but I was crying with pain, not celebrating! Then I saw our goalie. He was running toward me! He hadn't noticed me because he'd been trying to see what was happening at the other goal. As soon as he saw I couldn't stand up, he called over the other players. When I showed them my ankle, they were shocked. They helped me off the field, called an ambulance, and waited with me until it arrived.

Luckily my ankle wasn't broken, it was just badly injured. When I got home, I was surprised to see my entire team there. They'd been waiting for me to celebrate winning the match!

2 Read the text again and answer the questions.

   1 Who do you think the author is? What do you know about him/her? _____

   2 What do you think about the author's friends' reaction? Do you think they were good friends? Why? _____

3 **ANALYZE** In the text, find two examples of:

   1 The simple past   _____was_____ _____

   2 The past continuous   _____ _____

   3 The past perfect   _____ _____

   4 The past perfect continuous _____ _____

   5 Which tense is used most? _____ _____

4 Circle the linking words in the story: _when, as soon as, then, until, while._

WRITING TIP: a story

- Think of a <u>simple</u> story.
- Write an outline of the main points in the story: the beginning, the middle, the end.
- We use past tenses to tell a story:
  - Use the simple past for most of the verbs.
  - Use the past continuous for descriptions and when one action is interrupted by another.
  - Use the past perfect for a past action that happened before another past action.
- Use linking words to connect the parts of the story.
- Try to use some adjectives and adverbs to make the story more interesting.

5 **PLAN** Here are the first lines of two stories. Choose ONE of the stories and write a plan. Use the Writing tip to help you.

- It was getting dark and late and my friends still hadn't arrived. Where were they?
- When I got home, I saw a mysterious package with my name on it. What could it be?

Beginning		
Middle		
End		

6 **PRODUCE** Write your story in about 150–200 words. Use your plan from Exercise 5.

LISTENING

1 🔊 **10.01** **Listen to the three conversations. Complete the sentences with one word.**

1 Marcus can't go running because he has a problem with his _____ .

2 Annabel wants to go shopping _____ her doctor's appointment.

3 Linda's going to the match on _____ while Louis is going to get the _____ .

DIALOGUE

2 🔊 **10.01** **Put the conversations in the correct order. Then listen again and check.**

Conversation 1

☐	Marcus	Yes, but I don't really like water.
☐	Marcus	I can't. My knees aren't very strong.
☐	Marcus	That's right, so I think it's going to be biking.
1	Marcus	My doctor says I need to do some more exercise.
☐	Milly	What about swimming? That's really good for the whole body.
☐	Milly	Oh. So you need to do something that's easier on your legs?
☐	Milly	Really? Why don't you take up running?

Conversation 2

☐	Annabel	Of course. Just make sure you're here by about three.
☐	Annabel	It's at 4:30.
☐	Annabel	No, I'm leaving before that because I want to do some shopping.
☐	Jaden	So you need to leave the house at about four?
1	Jaden	What time's your doctor appointment tomorrow?
☐	Jaden	Can I get a ride with you?

Conversation 3

☐	Louis	I'm going to take the bus. I'll see you there.
1	Louis	Are you going to the game tomorrow?
☐	Louis	The car? Are you crazy? There won't be anywhere to park.
☐	Linda	Yes, I thought I'd take the car.
☐	Linda	So I'll walk then. It's always good to get some exercise.

> **PRONUNCIATION**
> /tʃ/ and /ʃ/ consonant sounds
> Go to page 121. 🎧

Train to TH!NK

Drawing conclusions

3 **Read the statements and check (✓) the correct conclusion.**

0 I like all fruits.
Apples are a fruit.
So …
I like apples. ✓
Apples are my favorite fruit. ☐

1 Math is the most popular subject at school.
I'm in math class.
So …
I'm doing my favorite class. ☐
Most people in my classroom are doing their favorite class. ☐

2 I only wear glasses to read.
I'm wearing my glasses.
So …
I'm reading a book. ☐
My eyes are tired. ☐

3 I need to go to bed at 8 p.m.
It's 10 p.m. and we're still out.
So …
I've forgotten what time it is. ☐
I'm tired. ☐

4 **Write conclusions for the statements.**

1 I always dance when I hear music.
I'm listening to a song on the radio.
So _____
_____

2 Robbie says yes to everything.
I asked Robbie if he wants a sandwich.
So _____
_____

3 His third book was his best.
His first book was better than his second book.
So _____
_____

4 My birthday is one day after Barney's.
Yesterday was Barney's birthday.
So _____
_____

B1 Preliminary for Schools

 READING

Part 3: Multiple-choice

1 **For each question choose the correct answer.**

1 What's Dan doing in the first paragraph?
- **A** explaining a process
- **B** encouraging people to be more active
- **C** describing his experience with half marathons and full marathons
- **D** discouraging people from running long distances

2 In the second paragraph, what does Dan say about running?
- **A** He's faster but his body suffers more.
- **B** He finds it more difficult to train and needs more time in between races.
- **C** He's only about ten minutes slower than his personal best from when he was younger.
- **D** He doesn't like the experience as much as he used to.

3 What does he enjoy most about races?
- **A** trying to run faster every time
- **B** the crowd encouraging him
- **C** seeing people who used to race, but don't any more
- **D** beating younger runners

4 Why does Dan visit schools?
- **A** to run races with the children
- **B** to talk about the history of marathon running
- **C** to encourage children to do sport
- **D** to show that old people can run fast

5 What might Dan write in his diary?
- **A** 'I started running a few years ago. I wanted to keep my body and mind young because I don't like getting old.'
- **B** 'When I was younger, I was really competitive but as I get older, I don't worry about how fast I go.'
- **C** 'I love the way running keeps me healthy and brings me into contact with so many people.'
- **D** 'Running became so difficult I nearly gave it up, but my doctor told me to keep going. I'm happy he did.'

Dan Collins: Half marathon runner

I started running half marathons a long time ago, when I was a teenager. A half marathon is 21 kilometres, by the way. I've tried a few full marathons, but 42 kilometres is a long way and I prefer the shorter distance. I'm almost 70 now, so I've been doing them for nearly 50 years, but I still get the same excitement at the beginning of each race as I used to.

I don't run as many half-marathons as I did. I used to run around 15 races every year and when I was in my thirties I got quite good at them. I think my personal best was around 1 hour 17 minutes, which was only ten minutes over the world record back then. These days I run about five races a year and my time is quite a bit slower. At my age you need a lot more preparation and your body doesn't recover as quickly, but it's well worth all the extra work.

There are two main reasons why I still run half marathons. Firstly, it means I'm keeping myself fit. My doctor told me that I'm healthier than most people half my age! But I think the real reason I love the sport so much is the other people you meet. You get to know other athletes and I've made many good friends over the years. The crowds of people who wait on the sides of the streets clapping and shouting as you run past are amazing. I get more and more support the older I get!

I now spend quite a lot of time visiting schools to get children interested in sport, especially running. I think it's really important to get involved at an early age. It makes it so much easier to keep doing it the older you get. The kids are always really keen and they ask me loads of questions. Many of them can't believe that I'm the same age as their grandfathers. Sometimes I invite them to run a five-kilometre race with me but not many of them can beat me!

EXAM GUIDE: READING PART 3

In B1 Preliminary for Schools Reading Part 3, you have to read a text and answer five multiple-choice questions. The questions are not about facts but opinions, attitudes and global and detailed meaning.

- Look at the title and read the text quickly.
- Don't worry too much about words you don't know. Try to get the general idea of their meaning from the context.
- The last question checks your understanding of <u>the whole text</u>.
- The other four questions are about parts of the text. These questions are in the same order as the information in the text.
- For questions 1, 2, 3, 4: read each question and find the part of the text that it refers to.
- Re-read the sentence(s) carefully and eliminate the options that you think are wrong.
- Read again and choose the correct answer.

CONSOLIDATION

🎧 LISTENING

1 🔊 **10.05** **Listen to the conversation. Check (✓) A, B, or C.**

1 What has Felicity's mother had problems with?
- **A** her back ☐
- **B** her foot ☐
- **C** her ankle ☐

2 Felicity's mother's problem has become worse because of
- **A** computers and tennis. ☐
- **B** tennis and the guitar. ☐
- **C** a new office job. ☐

3 What does Felicity's mother want to do?
- **A** work for a travel agency ☐
- **B** be a cooking teacher ☐
- **C** work in a restaurant ☐

2 🔊 **10.05** **Listen again. Mark the sentences T (true) or F (false).**

0 Felicity knows that her mother's operation was successful. | F |

1 Felicity's mother doesn't know how to use a computer. ☐

2 Felicity's mother used to play a lot of sports. ☐

3 Felicity's mother told her employers that she's leaving. ☐

4 Damon thinks that being a cook is fairly easy. ☐

5 Felicity's mother will earn less at her new job. ☐

🔤 VOCABULARY

3 **Match the parts of the sentences.**

0 I think you should make | c |

1 I'm sure you'll feel better if you get ☐

2 The test was easy. I finished it in ☐

3 I kept working at the problem ☐

4 I left the exam room as soon as ☐

5 It was a difficult question, but in ☐

6 You're sick? Oh, I really hope you get ☐

a until I got the right answer.
b I'd finished the test.
c an appointment to see a doctor.
d the end I found the right answer.
e better soon.
f some exercise.
g under an hour.

4 **Complete the sentences.**

0 The work's hard, but the p_ay_____ is really good, so I don't mind.

1 She works very hard, but she doesn't e_____ a lot, so it's difficult for her.

2 He did really well in the job and after six months he was p_____ .

3 I love travel, so I want to have a c_____ in tourism.

4 I didn't enjoy the work very much, so after a year I handed in my n_____ .

5 She left the job because the work wasn't c_____ enough for her.

🅖 GRAMMAR

5 **Rewrite the sentences. Use the words in parentheses.**

0 They don't pay us a lot. (aren't)
We aren't paid a lot.

1 They built a new school. (was)
_____

2 They have promoted my sister. (been)
_____

3 They are making another movie about the *Titanic*. (made)
_____

4 They show soccer on TV every day! (shown)
_____

5 They have knocked down that building. (been)
_____

6 **Complete the text. Use the simple past, past perfect, or past perfect continuous of the verbs.**

One day, my uncle ⁰_____*left*_____ (leave) work very late – about 7:30 p.m. He ¹_____ (be) very tired because he ²_____ (spend) the whole afternoon writing emails. When he left, he ³_____ (write) emails for more than three hours! He ⁴_____ (start) to drive home, but he got stuck in a lot of traffic because there ⁵_____ (be) a very bad accident at seven o'clock. When he finally ⁶_____ (get) home, it was 9:40 – he ⁷_____ (drive) for almost two hours. Then he ⁸_____ (realize) that he couldn't get into his house because he ⁹_____ (leave) his keys on his desk in the office!

DIALOGUE

7 **10.06** **Complete the conversation with the phrases in the list. Then listen again and check.**

> as long as | as soon as | by the way
> for a while | hadn't been | have an operation
> in a few weeks' time | ~~sounds great~~

Nick So, how was your weekend?

Marta Really nice, thanks. On Sunday, I went for a picnic with my family.

Nick ⁰ _Sounds great_ . I love picnics. ¹_____, how is your little brother? Someone told me that he ²_____ very well.

Marta Well, that's right. He was pretty sick ³_____ . The doctor said that he might need to ⁴_____ . But that didn't happen, I'm happy to say. And he's OK now, thanks. He has to go back to the doctor ⁵_____ , but ⁶_____ he looks after himself, things should be OK.

Nick Has he gone back to school yet?

Marta Not yet. But he'll go back ⁷_____ he feels well enough, maybe next week. He really misses it.

Nick Really? Wow, I'd love a few weeks off school!

📖 READING

8 **Read the article. Write the paragraph titles in the correct places. There are two titles you don't need.**

> ~~Get close to nature~~ | Go running | Keep moving
> Think about food | Surf the internet
> Use your work area as a gym | Walk to work
> Watch how you sit

✏️ WRITING

9 **Write a paragraph (about 120–150 words) about how you can keep healthy at school. Use the ideas to help you:**

- getting to school
- food
- exercise
- the way you sit / stand / walk

HOW CAN PEOPLE STAY HEALTHY AT WORK?

The working week can be long and tiring, but did you know that the workplace can be unhealthy in different ways? People can make some simple changes to their work routine to make it healthier.

⓪ _Get close to nature_
It has been shown that a 30–50-minute walk in a park can improve your work performance by about 20 percent.

1 _____
Yes, really! In an experiment with 96 students, the ones who were allowed to use the internet during a ten-minute break were found to work better afterwards.

2 _____
It's possible to find exercises you can do in your chair or using your desk that will help you stay in better shape.

3 _____
Sitting down all day isn't very healthy. It can cause back pains, for example. It's always good to get up sometimes and walk around the office. Try not to sit still for too long.

4 _____
It's easy to just get a sandwich from the machine, but it's much better to bring fresh food that has been prepared at home. Oh, and water, too – that's really important. Drink a lot of it.

5 _____
A lot of people spend hours working in front of a computer. Back pain and wrist problems are easily caused this way. The way you sit is very important. Keep your back and shoulders straight when you are sitting at your desk and make sure the screen is at eye level.

11 BREAKING NEWS

Grammar rap!

G GRAMMAR
Reported statements

→ SB p.104

1 ⭐☆☆ **Put the words in order to make sentences.**

0 that / said / She / only / it / joke / was / a
She said that it was only a joke.

1 could / me / me / He / help / he / told / that
_____

2 they / said / lunch / join / would / They / for / us
_____

3 late / I / that / be / was / I / going / you / told / to
_____

4 said / before / article / the / The / had / accident / day / the / happened
_____

5 she / teacher / Our / had / told / lost / us / homework / our
_____

2 ⭐⭐⭐ **Write reported statements.**

0 Jason: "I'm going to buy a scooter."
Jason said _____*he was going to buy a scooter.*

1 Emily to me: "I want to go to the concert."
Emily told _____

2 Lauren: "I wasn't happy with the test."
Lauren said _____

3 Zoe to Micky: "I haven't seen that movie yet."
Zoe told _____

4 Alec: "We'll be late unless we leave soon."
Alec said _____

5 Scarlett to Dan: "I didn't really enjoy the party."
Scarlett told _____

6 Jack: "I wasn't feeling very well."
Jack said _____

7 Bella to Jo: "I don't want to invite Tim to my party."
Bella told _____

3 ⭐⭐⭐ **Read the email. Then complete the conversation.**

✈ **Isla**
Isla@thinkmail.com

Hi Isla,

Just a quick message to say that Seville is great! We got here three days ago and we're staying in a hotel not far from the famous Real Alcázar, a group of really beautiful palaces with a famous gallery. We visited it on the first day and I was very impressed by it. We've seen a lot of fascinating sights so far – I liked the Giralda Tower most. Now we're going to spend time in the Plaza de España. I am so looking forward to this. I've heard it's one of the most beautiful squares in Spain, with a canal and bridges that look like the ones in Venice!

Tomorrow we're going to Cáceres. Mom's a bit worried because we'll be in the car for more than four hours. But Dad says it's a fascinating city – it was built by the Romans more than 2,000 years ago! That's it from me. Next week we're off to France!

Hope you're OK.

Love, Ruby

Isla I got an email from Ruby last week. She's on vacation with her parents in Seville in Spain. She said they ⁰ ____*had*____ gotten there two days before, and they ¹ _____ in a hotel near a famous palace. She said they ² _____ it on their first day and she ³ _____ really impressed by it.

Ellie I've heard that Seville's a beautiful city.

Isla That's right. Ruby told me that she ⁴ _____ a lot of fascinating sights like the Giralda Tower and a beautiful square, the Plaza de España.

Ellie Where's she going next?

Isla She said they ⁵ _____ to Cáceres next.

Verb patterns: object + infinitive → SB p.107

4 ★☆☆ **Match the parts of the sentences.**

0 They said the mountain was dangerous and ☐ *f*
1 She invited us to stay at their ☐
2 I was very tired, but John ☐
3 The tickets were expensive, but they ☐
4 Logan is a great soccer player. They picked ☐
5 It'll be cold tonight, so Jess reminded me to ☐
6 I'm not too sure about my Spanish, but my ☐
7 Ms. Miller told us to study harder, and we ☐

a persuaded me to stay up for a few more hours.
b allowed us to get in without standing in line.
c him to play on the school's all-star team.
d bring some warm clothes.
e teacher always encourages me to speak in class.
f warned us not to climb it without a good guide.
g asked her to explain the grammar again.
h place for the weekend.

5 ★★☆ **Complete the conversations. Use the correct patterns of the verbs.**

0 **A** What did Sean want from you?
  B Oh, he _____*wanted me to help*_____ (want / help) him in the garden.
1 **A** Why didn't you take the four o'clock bus, guys?
  B Our friends _____ (persuade / stay) a bit longer.
2 **A** I've heard you aren't coming to the park with us.
  B No. Mom _____ (ask / help) her with the grocery shopping.
3 **A** Why didn't you watch the movie at home?
  B Our neighbors _____ (invite / watch) it on their big screen TV.
4 **A** Why aren't you coming into the yard?
  B Well, my friends have _____ (warn / not get) too close to your dog.
5 **A** Is Alice a good swimmer?
  B Yes. They've just _____ (pick / be) the captain of the school team.
6 **A** Your sister came in second in the race!
  B Yes, that's right. I _____ (not expect / do) so well.
7 **A** Why didn't Charlie go out on Thursday night?
  B His parents _____ (not allow / go out) except on weekends.

PRONUNCIATION
Polite intonation Go to page 121.

6 ★★★ **Rewrite the sentences. Say what happened. Use the verbs.**

0 Lizzie: "Jon, would you like to see a movie?" (invite)
  Lizzie invited Jon to see a movie.
1 Poppy: "Kitty, can you help me please?" (ask)
  _____
2 Elliot: "You should join the band, Mia." (encourage)
  _____
3 Alex: "Meet me at six o'clock, Dylan." (tell)
  _____
4 Mr. Jones: "Gabriela! Don't go into the water!" (warn)
  _____
5 Dexter's dad: "Don't forget to feed the cat, Dexter." (remind)
  _____

7 ★★★ **Complete the conversations. Use the verbs to disagree.**

0 **A** Here are your peaches. (ask)
  B But _____*I asked you to buy some vegetables!*_____
1 **A** You did Exercise 2. That's wrong. (tell)
  B But you _____
2 **A** I forgot your memory stick. (remind)
  B But I _____
3 **A** He fell out of the tree and broke his leg. (warn)
  B But I _____
4 **A** You didn't come to my party! (not invite)
  B But you _____

GET IT *RIGHT!*

Verb tenses with *ask*, *say*, and *tell*

Learners sometimes use the wrong tenses with *ask*, *say*, and *tell*.

✓ I **told** her I could help.
✗ I ~~tell~~ her I could help.

Correct the sentences.

0 When I heard the news, I ask if it was true.
  When I heard the news, I asked if it was true.
1 She says she'd call me yesterday, but she didn't.
  _____
2 We invited Beth and tell her to bring pizza.
  _____
3 I'm so happy that you ask me to write the article.
  _____
4 Tomorrow, I ask a friend about the homework.
  _____
5 Danny, I already tell them that you're coming tonight.
  _____

VOCABULARY
Fun

→ SB p.104

1 ★☆☆ **Complete the conversations with "fun" words.**

0 A Why can't you go to the office like this?
  B Everybody will __laugh at me__ .

1 A Hahahaha!
  B It isn't _____ . Stop laughing, please.

2 A Did you enjoy the birthday party?
  B Oh, yes. It was so much _____ .

3 A I didn't like the movie at all.
  B I thought it was _____ . I couldn't stop laughing.

4 A Why do people _____ of her?
  B I'm not sure, but I think it's really mean.

5 A I didn't _____ .
  B I know what you mean. It's never easy to understand jokes in another language.

6 A Erin's really good at telling _____ .
  B Yes, she always makes me laugh.

7 A Should we play a _____ on Dad?
  B Yes! Let's hide his newspaper.

More verbs with object + infinitive

→ SB p.107

2 ★★☆ **Match the parts of the sentences.**

0 I warned them not to | f |
1 My English teacher persuaded me to | |
2 I wasn't expecting you to be home | |
3 My parents don't allow my little sister to | |
4 He's very shy. I think we should encourage | |
5 Can I remind you to buy | |
6 Can we invite you to come | |
7 Nicole wanted me to | |

a him to join the youth center.
b watch TV at all. They think it's bad for her.
c to our place on Saturday?
d read out a story to the whole class.
e so early.
f be late.
g tell her the answers.
h some vegetables for lunch?

3 ★★☆ **Complete the sentences with the correct form of the verbs in the list.**

> encourage | expect | warn | invite
> not allow | remind | want

0 Our teacher __encouraged__ us to enter the competition.

1 Joe's parents _____ him to stay out late.

2 Nobody _____ Sonya to win the race. It was a surprise.

3 What do you _____ us to do with these books?

4 Lois _____ the whole class to her party.

5 The sign _____ everyone not to go in the water.

6 I _____ you to call the dentist and you forgot!

WordWise: Expressions with *make*

→ SB p.105

4 ★☆☆ Circle the correct words.

0 This story is too good to be true. I'm sure they made it *off* / *up* / *on* / *down*.

1 Let me make *good* / *fun* / *easy* / *sure* I understand.

2 He didn't even apologize. That made us really *angry* / *cool* / *easy* / *worse*.

3 Good teachers can make a *desire* / *distance* / *damage* / *difference* in students' lives.

4 I know her, but I've never made *students* / *friends* / *partners* / *colleagues* with her.

5 Don't make *jokes* / *fun* / *laughter* / *play* of me.

5 ★★☆ **Match the questions with the replies.**

0 Should we do that now or tomorrow? | d |
1 Can I borrow $10? | |
2 Why don't you like them? | |
3 What did you think of the book? | |
4 Is this really what happened? | |
5 When did you make friends? | |

a OK, but make sure you pay me back.
b Because they make fun of me all the time.
c Of course not. They made it up.
d You choose. It makes no difference to me.
e A long time ago. We went to school together.
f It made me really happy.

6 ★★★ **Answer the questions.**

1 What makes you angry?

_____

2 Have you ever read a news story that was made up?

_____

3 Do sports make a difference in your life?

_____

REFERENCE

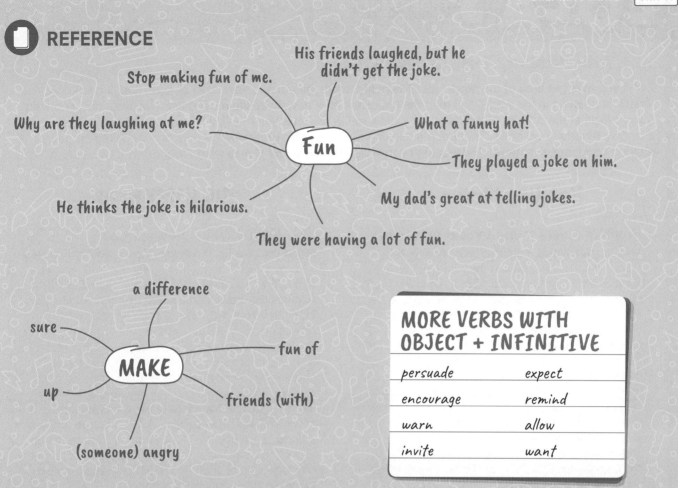

Stop making fun of me.

His friends laughed, but he didn't get the joke.

Why are they laughing at me?

Fun

What a funny hat!

They played a joke on him.

My dad's great at telling jokes.

He thinks the joke is hilarious.

They were having a lot of fun.

a difference

sure

MAKE

fun of

up

friends (with)

(someone) angry

MORE VERBS WITH OBJECT + INFINITIVE

persuade	expect
encourage	remind
warn	allow
invite	want

VOCABULARY *EXTRA*

1 Circle the correct words.

1 to *crack* / *have* a joke
2 to have a *blast* / *fun*
3 to be able to take a *joke* / *fun*
4 an *inside* / *outside* joke
5 to take all the *fun* / *funny* out of it
6 You must be *joking* / *cracking*!

2 Complete the sentences with the correct form of the phrases in Exercise 1.

0 The neighbors complained we were making too much noise at the party, so we had to be quiet.
It _____took all the fun out of it_____ .

1 When we arrived everyone was really quiet. But Eva _____ and after that we were all laughing and having fun.

2 **A** I just heard you've won first prize in the talent competition.
B Me? _____ .
I don't believe it!

3 Sam's so serious and got upset when I played a joke on him. He isn't _____ .

4 The comedy show we went to was absolutely amazing. We couldn't stop laughing. Everyone was _____ .

5 My best friend and I have so many _____ that only we understand and find funny – true friendship!

...... AND FINALLY, SOME GOOD NEWS!

Don't you ever get tired of the news? It's always the same thing these days: bad or fake. I do like to know what's happening in the world, so I read the headlines on a news website most days. The other day, I noticed a tiny article at the bottom of the page. Why did it catch my attention? Well, it was about a news website that only reports good news! That got me thinking there must be other newspapers and websites out there sharing good, positive news. And wouldn't you believe it, there are! Here's what I found:

Positive.News

Positive News website and magazine

The **Positive News** magazine website says it reports what's going right in the world, not what's wrong with it. That's a good start! It reminded me of other news websites – until I started reading. The day's main news stories are always there, but with the difference that they concentrate on progress, new possibilities, and solutions. They call this *constructive journalism* and it certainly makes a difference. This is the news site to go to if you want to find out what's happening in the world without feeling depressed!

The daily news is divided into sections: society, lifestyle, environment, science, economics, opinion, and local and world news, so it's very easy to navigate. It also looks very professional with great photographs and interesting, honest articles.

As well as the website, *Positive News* magazine is printed four times a year. The modern design and amazing photos made me turn the pages quickly to see what was next. The magazine hopes to make its readers feel good and remind them about the good things happening around the world. It certainly had that effect on me!

THE HAPPY NEWS

The Happy News newspaper

When you pick up **The Happy News**, you immediately see it's different from other newspapers. Just looking at it makes you feel better! It's colorful and all the pictures are drawn and colored by hand. The text is in bright boxes, circles, and stars. Its relaxed, friendly design certainly encouraged me to read it.

The Happy News was the idea of Emily Coxhead, a young artist from the north of England. She was getting depressed by the non-stop bad news in the media so she created her own newspaper to share the good things that happen and celebrate the actions of wonderful people. The newspaper contains articles about positive stories from around the world as well as a section called "Everyday Heroes" about ordinary people, or groups of people, who do things to make other people's lives better.

The Happy News is printed on paper – there's a website, too – and it comes out every three months. It has been so successful that the brand now includes birthday cards, books, and bags, all designed by Emily. It looks like I'm not the only one who wants some good news!

📖 READING

1 Read the article and answer the questions.

1 What is Lola tired of?

_____

2 What sort of news does she want to read?

_____

3 Which newspaper do you think she liked best? Why?

_____

2 Read the text again. Mark the sentences PN (Positive News), HN (Happy News), or B (both).

0 It is full of fun and happiness. _HN_
1 It has articles about special people. _____
2 You can read about today's world events. _____
3 There's a print version available. _____
4 It has articles on many different topics. _____
5 It looks very attractive. _____
6 There are other products apart from the newspaper / magazine. _____
7 It has suggestions on how situations can be improved. _____

3 CRITICAL THINKING Match the headlines (a–f) with the news sections (1–6).

1 Economics [f]
2 Environment [ ]
3 Everyday heroes [ ]
4 Lifestyle [ ]
5 Science [ ]
6 World news [ ]

a Walking is good for your body and mind.
b The 3-D printer that can make a new heart.
c Number of rare butterflies is going up.
d Global leaders agree on climate change plan.
e Teens put out fire in old people's home.
f Green money: the best accounts for savings.

DEVELOPING } *Writing*

A report for the school magazine

1 **INPUT** Read the report and write what the numbers refer to.

0 1997 *The year the Guggenheim Museum was created.*

1 11,000 _____

2 five _____

3 24,000 _____

The day we visited a museum – in cyberspace!

A Last week's art classes were very different from normal. We were pretty excited when Mr. Breen, our teacher, told us to choose a museum in a different country to visit online. He also said that we should write an article for the school magazine about it.

B There were five of us in my group and it wasn't easy to decide which museum to choose. Mr. Breen encouraged us to make one suggestion each. We had five suggestions, but everybody voted for Thomas's idea: the Guggenheim Museum in Bilbao, Spain. When he showed us the website, we all knew it was the museum for us.

C The building was created by American architect Frank Gehry in 1997 and it's amazing. The website says it covers an area of 24,000 m², including 11,000 m² of exhibition space. It took us about two hours to visit the whole website and our favorite part was the Explore section. We enjoyed looking at the excellent photos of art in the various exhibitions in the museum.

D When the project was finished, Mia, from our group, said what we all felt. She said that the project had been fascinating, but what we'd really like now is to travel to Bilbao to visit the Guggenheim!

Mathilda Walton, Class 6A

2 Complete the sentences from the report with the missing verb forms.

1 Our teacher told us _____ a museum in a different country.

2 Everybody _____ for Thomas's idea: the Guggenheim Museum in Bilbao, Spain.

3 Mia said the project _____ fascinating, but what we _____ really like to do now is visit the Guggenheim in Bilbao.

3 **ANALYZE** Read the text again. Match the descriptions (1–4) with the paragraphs (A–D).

Which paragraph

1 gives the students' opinion of the project? ☐

2 is about how the students chose a museum to visit? ☐

3 explains the project? ☐

4 describes the museum and gives details about it? ☐

WRITING TIP: a report

- Choose a good title to catch the readers' attention.
- Start with an interesting first line.
- Include some facts and interesting details.
- Use reported speech when you write about what people said.
- Remember to write a final comment about the event/experience.
- Write in a neutral style, neither formal nor informal.

4 **PLAN** You are going to write a report for your school magazine. Choose a recent event at your school and write a plan. Use the Writing tip to help you.

Don't forget to include:
- the details of the event: When? Where? Why? Who?
- what happened and what you did
- people's reactions and comments

5 **PRODUCE** Write a report for your school magazine in about 200 words. Use your plan from Exercise 4.

 **LISTENING**

1 🔊 **11.03** Listen to the three conversations. (Circle) the correct words.

  1 Leo and Rosie *agree / disagree* about the problem.

  2 Sam *encourages / discourages* Anya to join the acting club.

  3 Max *refuses / accepts* Layla's advice.

2 🔊 **11.03** Listen again and answer the questions.

Conversation 1

  0 Where are Leo and Rosie?
    They're in a park.

  1 Why is Leo angry?
    _____

  2 What does Leo think the police should do?
    _____

Conversation 2

  3 How does Anya feel about joining the club?
    _____

  4 What happened at her old school?
    _____

  5 How does Sam feel about what the boy said?
    _____

Conversation 3

  6 Why is Max upset?
    _____

  7 What does Layla think he should do?
    _____

  8 Why can't Max do that?
    _____

3 🔊 **11.03** Match the questions and statements (1–6) with the responses (a–f). Then listen again and check.

  1 What's up, Leo? | a |

  2 I get really angry when I see something like this. ☐

  3 He always said I was a hopeless actor. ☐

  4 What really counts is that you enjoy what you do and want to become better. ☐

  5 How do you know Harry's telling the truth? ☐

  6 You need to go and talk to Finn now. ☐

  a Just look at the mess over there.

  b Me too. This is awful.

  c That's right. You know what? I think I'll give it a try and join the club.

  d I don't. But I can't go and ask Finn.

  e Seriously? I get so angry when people say things like that.

  f You know what? You're absolutely right, Layla.

DIALOGUE

4 🔊 **11.04** Put the conversation in the correct order. Then listen and check.

  ☐ **Martin** But just imagine if that really worked! I think I'll ask my science teacher about it.

  ☐ **Martin** I'm just saying I'll talk to my science teacher. Don't shout at me.

  [1] **Martin** Hey, Alison, check this out. The paper says this guy has just discovered how to produce gasoline out of nothing.

  ☐ **Alison** I'm telling you – it's not worth it. It's all complete nonsense.

  ☐ **Alison** Out of nothing? I think we're talking about fake news here.

  ☐ **Alison** Sorry, I didn't mean to be rude. Of course you can have a word with your science teacher. See what she thinks.

(2 hours later)

  ☐ **Martin** She was like, "You shouldn't believe everything you see in a newspaper!"

  ☐ **Martin** Yeah, I know.

  ☐ **Alison** See? I told you.

  ☐ **Alison** So what did she say?

PHRASES FOR FLUENCY   → SB p.108

5 Complete the conversations with the phrases in the list.

> check this out | have a word
> I'm just saying | it's not worth it
> ~~was like~~ | we're talking about

  0 **A** How did she react when she heard she'd won first prize?

    B She _____ *was like* _____ , "Me? I can't believe it's true!"

  1 **A** I said sorry to Anne, but she ignored me.

    B Yes, _____ . She never forgives anyone.

  2 **A** _____ . It's a message I got this morning.

    B Strange. Who would write something like this?

  3 **A** I'm angry with Jorge. I'm not inviting him to my party.

    B But _____ your best friend. Maybe you should have a talk with him.

  4 **A** Do you really need another scarf?

    B Yes, I do. Anyway, why are you so interested?

    A _____ you already have too many.

  5 **A** Megan seems upset and I don't know why.

    B I think you should _____ with her after school.

B1 Preliminary for Schools

 **WRITING**
Part 2: Choice between an article or a story

1 **Choose one of these questions.**

Write your answer in about 100 words.

Question 1

You see this notice in an English-language magazine.

Articles wanted!
Great magazines

What makes a great magazine?
Is it the photos, the articles, the interviews with famous people –
or all of these things?
Recommend a magazine you enjoy reading.
Tell us why you like it!

Write an article answering these questions and we will
publish the most interesting articles on our website.

Write your **article**.

Question 2

- Your English teacher has asked you to write a story.
- Your story must begin with this sentence:

  I opened the newspaper and there was a photo of me on page 2.

Write your **story**.

EXAM GUIDE: WRITING PART 2

In B1 Preliminary for Schools Writing Part 2, you have to write <u>one</u> text. You can choose an article or a story.

- Read the two questions carefully and choose the one you think you can do best.
- Take a few minutes to make a plan.
- **The article**: make sure you answer <u>all</u> the questions in the task.

  Make sure your article is well organised and contains relevant information.

  The story: your story must start with the sentence given in the task.

  Make sure your story has clear links to the first sentence.

  You usually write a story using past tenses.
- Re-read your article/story to check your grammar and spelling.
- Don't write too many or too few words. Write about 100 words.

12 RULES AND REGULATIONS

Grammar rap!

▶ 35

 GRAMMAR
be allowed to / let

 SB p.112

1 ★☆☆ **Match the sentences with the pictures.**

0 They don't let you play ball games here. `C`
1 You're allowed to swim here. ☐
2 You aren't allowed to use your phone here. ☐
3 They rode their bikes, but they weren't allowed to. ☐
4 You aren't allowed to take photos here. ☐
5 You aren't allowed to take food into the museum. ☐

2 ★☆☆ **Complete the sentences with *let(s)*
or *allowed*.**

0 Dad ____*lets*____ me help him when he cooks.
1 I'm not _____ to go out on weekday evenings.
2 Are you _____ to use your phone
at mealtimes?
3 My parents don't _____ me have a pet.
4 Does your dad _____ you use his camera?
5 I'm _____ to use my mom's tablet.

3 ★★☆ **Look at the information about Jason's
school. Write the rules with *let* or *allowed*.**

OK!	NOT OK!
• wearing sneakers	• eating during class
• forgetting homework once a month	• running in the hall
• sending work by email	• using phones in class
• using tablets	• borrowing more than three books from the library

0 *Students are allowed to wear sneakers.*
1 The teachers let them _____
2 _____
3 _____
4 _____
5 _____
6 _____
7 _____

4 ★★☆ **Complete the conversation with *be
allowed to* or *let* and the verbs in the list.**

call | change | chew | do
listen | make | take | take | use

Oscar So how do you like it here, Grace?
Grace It's OK, but it's different from my old school.
Oscar You mean you ⁰ *aren't allowed to do*
things that you could do at your old school?
Grace Well, not really, but the rules are different. At
my old school, we ¹_____ cell
phones into the classroom, but here it's OK.
Oscar Oh, I see. Well, they ²_____ us
_____ smartphones to check
things online, but we ³_____
calls.
Grace Oh, I see. ⁴_____
they _____ us
_____ someone at break?
Oscar Sure, that's no problem.
Grace And do they ⁵_____ us
_____ to music in class?
Oscar Of course not.
Grace The teachers at my old school
⁶_____ us
_____ our tablets into class.
Oscar Wow! That's amazing!
Grace And they ⁷_____ us
_____ gum.
Oscar I should ask my parents to
⁸_____ me
_____ to your old school!

5 ★★★ **Write sentences about what you are or
aren't allowed to do at your school.**

PRONUNCIATION
Silent consonants Go to page 121.

Third conditional

→ SB p.115

6 ★★☆ **Match the texts (0–5) with the sentences (a–f).**

0 We were the better team and the score was 2–1, with us winning. We had another three minutes to play and I was so nervous. Then I caught the ball with my hands, right in front of our goal! `d`

1 My mom told me I should be careful with my money. But I didn't think. I spent it all on snacks and after a week it was all gone. ☐

2 I was three years old. I knew I wasn't allowed to climb the ladder in my grandpa's yard. But I did and I had a bad accident. ☐

3 They were late for the train. They ran as fast as they could, but missed it and had to wait for two hours. ☐

4 It was awful. I didn't want to hurt Lottie, but I was so stressed out. She asked me if I could help her and I gave her a very unfriendly answer. ☐

5 I'm sorry I woke you up, Lily. I didn't know you were sick. ☐

a If they'd left earlier, they wouldn't have gotten home so late.

b He'd have been friendlier if he'd been more relaxed.

c He wouldn't have broken his leg if he hadn't done that.

d If he hadn't touched the ball with his hands, his team would have won.

e If she'd listened, she wouldn't have bought all those snacks.

f She wouldn't have called her so early if somebody had told her about the situation.

7 ★★☆ **Complete the sentences with the correct form of the verbs.**

0 If I had started to play the piano a few years ago, I _would have played_ (play) at the concert.

1 If I _____ (read) my messages this morning, I'd have answered you right away.

2 If it had been warmer, they _____ (eat) on the patio.

3 We _____ (not lose) our way if the GPS had worked.

4 If I _____ (not study) so much, I wouldn't have done well on my test.

5 Would you have lost the game if you _____ (not be) so nervous?

6 He _____ (not buy) the bike if the price hadn't been so low.

7 If Gemma's friends had texted her, _____ she _____ (join) them?

8 ★★★ **Write third conditional sentences.**

0 On Sunday it was raining, so Joshua got up late.
If it hadn't been raining, Joshua wouldn't have
got up late.

1 He didn't hear the phone. Rory didn't talk to him.
_____

2 Joshua was by himself all afternoon. He was bored.
_____

3 He went to bed at 6 p.m. He woke up at midnight.
_____

4 He didn't go back to sleep. He was tired on Monday.
_____

5 He was tired. He found the math test difficult.
_____

6 Joshua got a bad grade. His teacher was disappointed.
_____

9 ★★★ **Write third conditional sentences that are true for you.**

0 _If I'd caught the bus, I'd have been on time._
1 If I hadn't _____
2 If I'd _____
3 If I hadn't _____

GET IT RIGHT!

Third conditional

Learners sometimes use the wrong tenses in the third conditional – either in the main clause or in the *if* clause.

✓ What **would have happened** if I hadn't been here?

✗ What ~~had happened~~ if I hadn't been here?

✓ If I **had seen** him, I would have said hello.

✗ If I ~~would have seen~~ him, I would have said hello.

Correct the sentences.

0 If you hadn't helped me, I won't finish my essay.
If you hadn't helped me, I wouldn't have finished
my essay.

1 If you'd have been there, it would have been fun.
_____

2 The trip would have been difficult if it would rain.
_____

3 It was worse if we hadn't gotten there on time.
_____

4 I'm sure you would have enjoyed it if you were there.
_____

5 If I hadn't brought my umbrella, I'd get wet.
_____

VOCABULARY
Discipline

→ SB p.112

1 ★☆☆ **Complete the sentences with the phrases in the list.**

> allowed to | get into trouble | let
> breaks the rules | gets told off
> do what you are told
> gets punished | behave well

0 When you're _____allowed to_____ do something, you get permission to do it.

1 When your teachers don't _____ you do something, you can't do it without getting into trouble.

2 When you _____ , you do what's expected of you.

3 When young children _____ , they act in a way that pleases other people.

4 When someone _____ , they feel the consequences of what they've done.

5 When someone _____ , they're doing something wrong.

6 When you _____ , you're in a difficult situation.

7 When someone _____ , another person speaks angrily to them.

2 ★★☆ **Complete the conversations with the phrases in Exercise 1. Use the correct form of the verbs and make any other necessary changes.**

0 **A** Did the thief _____get punished_____ ?
   B Yes, of course. He'll be in prison for three years.

1 **A** Did your brother _____ you borrow his tablet?
   B No. I took it without asking him.

2 **A** What was that shouting?
   B Luke _____ by Dad because he ran into the living room with dirty shoes on.

3 **A** Are you _____ use your dad's laptop without asking?
   B No. I always have to ask first.

4 **A** Why can't I see Tommy anymore?
   B Because you always _____ when you're with him.

5 **A** Your little sister is so nice. Does she always _____ ?
   B Only when she's with other people. Otherwise she can be a pain.

6 **A** Nadia, go and do your homework.
   B Mom, can I go out and do it tomorrow?
   A No, Nadia. _____ !

3 ★★★ **Complete the sentences so that they are true for you.**

1 When I behave well,
_____

2 My parents never let me
_____

3 I always get told off when I
_____

4 If you break the school rules,
_____

5 When I get into trouble, I
_____

6 I'm only allowed to
_____

Talking about consequences and reasons

→ SB p.115

4 ★☆☆ **Match the parts of the conversations.**

0 Last summer was the hottest one ever. | g |
1 You forgot Holly's birthday yesterday. | |
2 I didn't get any sleep last night. | |
3 So you're working late tonight? | |
4 Bonnie broke her leg two days ago. | |
5 Henry got into trouble at school. | |
6 I just don't have any money. | |

a That's why you're in such a bad mood today.
b Yes. It was because of his bad behavior.
c That explains why she hasn't been at school.
d So that's why you don't want to come shopping with me.
e Yes, and that's why I can't join you for dinner.
f So that's the reason why she isn't talking to me.
g It's definitely because of climate change.

5 ★★★ **Complete the sentences so that they are true for you.**

1 I'm learning English because _____

2 _____ because of the weather.

3 This weekend I have to _____ and that's why _____

4 Where I live, most people _____ and that explains why _____
_____
_____

REFERENCE

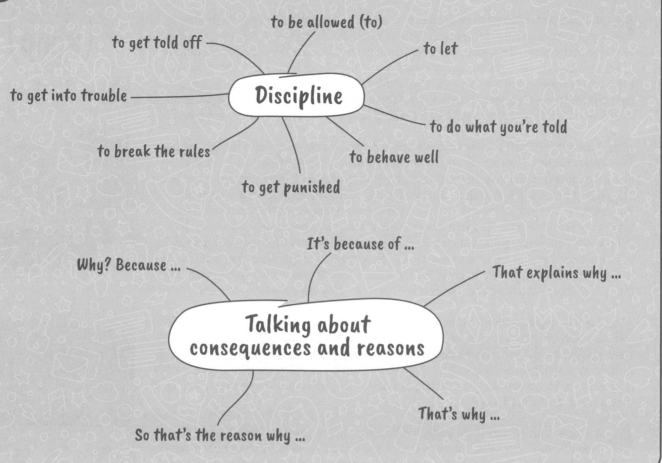

to be allowed (to)

to get told off

to let

to get into trouble — Discipline

to do what you're told

to break the rules

to behave well

to get punished

It's because of ...

Why? Because ...

That explains why ...

Talking about consequences and reasons

So that's the reason why ...

That's why ...

VOCABULARY *EXTRA*

1 Mark the phrases P (positive) or N (negative).

0 [N] behave badly
1 ☐ be good
2 ☐ play by the rules
3 ☐ be given detention
4 ☐ be given another chance
5 ☐ get caught

2 Match the sentences with the correct form of the phrases in Exercise 1.

a Harriet <u>was seen doing something wrong</u>. [5]
   Harriet _____*got caught.*_____

b Noah always <u>behaves well</u>. ☐
   Noah _____ always _____

c The teacher <u>made us stay behind after class</u>. ☐
   The teacher _____

d The children <u>didn't do what they were told</u>. ☐
   The children _____

e He didn't hand in his homework on time,
   but the teacher said he <u>could hand it in tomorrow</u>. ☐
   He didn't hand in his homework on time,
   but the teacher said he _____

f If they <u>hadn't cheated</u>, they would have lost. ☐
   If they _____, they would have lost.

FOOD FOR THOUGHT

A Is it ever acceptable to break rules and laws in society? What if doing so means helping people who are in need? Should people get into trouble for trying to deal with one of the world's biggest problems? One in nine people doesn't have enough to eat, but can you believe that approximately one third of all food produced around the world is wasted and that almost 50% of the fruit and vegetables we grow are destroyed? There are a lot of reasons why food is wasted and one of the main ones is that supermarkets and stores remove food from sale a few days before its sell-by date.

B A lot of food that is thrown out like this is perfectly safe to eat and there have been many cases of workers taking it from the trash and giving it away to people in need. According to the law, this is stealing and these workers have gotten into trouble. They didn't believe they had done anything wrong. Quite the opposite, they thought they were being kind. After all, if the supermarkets and store owners had wanted the food, they wouldn't have thrown it away. But is it a crime? Food waste activists don't believe so. They believe that wasting food is the real crime and they regularly take food from the trash outside stores and restaurants as a protest. In this way, they want to bring the problem to the attention of the public and lawmakers. However, until recently, many activists risked fines and punishment because they were breaking the law.

C It is still illegal to take food from the trash in some countries, but a lot of countries are now changing their laws. France was one of the first countries to introduce a law against food waste: stores and restaurants are not allowed to throw extra food away. Instead, they have to give it to charities. In Norway and Australia, the government is trying to cut food waste in half. And in South Korea, people now have to pay money if they want to throw food away.

D A success story in the fight against food waste in the UK is the FoodCycle initiative. At FoodCycle, volunteers cook tasty meals with extra food from stores and supermarkets. Volunteers and guests come together to enjoy a healthy meal and a talk. Guests include lonely or elderly people, poor families, and people without jobs or homes. At FoodCycle's 38 centers around the UK, they have now served more than one million meals! That's 425 tons of extra food that would have gone to waste if they hadn't used it! This is a great initiative, but it is still more expensive for supermarkets to donate their extra food than to throw it away. Many people believe the laws should be changed to fix this problem.

 READING

1 Read the article. Match the photos with the paragraphs.

2 Read the article again and answer the questions.

    0 What types of food are wasted the most?
    fruit and vegetables

    1 What is one of the main reasons so much food is wasted?
    _____

    2 Why don't food workers feel bad about taking food from the trash?
    _____

    3 What is a new rule in South Korea about food waste?
    _____

    4 How is FoodCycle helping to solve the food waste problem?
    _____

3 **CRITICAL THINKING** Look at these sentences. Which person might say them? Pick people from the list.

> an activist | a food worker | a lawmaker
> a person in need | a supermarket manager

0 I was only trying to help. If I'd known it was illegal, I wouldn't have taken it.
a food worker

1 I didn't let you take that. I told you to put it in the trash. You are stealing.
_____

2 You should give it to a charity for the homeless. They need it.
_____

3 But it was in the trash and I'm hungry. I don't have any money.
_____

4 It is against the law to destroy extra food. It must be given to charity.
_____

DEVELOPING *Writing*

A (light-hearted) set of rules

1 **INPUT** **Read the rules and answer the questions.**

   1 Are the rules serious? How do you know?

   2 What is the punishment if you break any of them?

MY "DREAM" RULES FOR THE SHOPPING MALL

1 The main purpose of the Arcade Shopping Mall is for teenagers to have a good time. Nobody is allowed to do anything that young people wouldn't like.

2 If a teen is tired or hungry, they're allowed to go to a café and they can eat and drink whatever they want without paying. If no seats are free, an adult has to stand up so a young person can sit down.

3 Nobody is allowed to tell teens not to run around or use their skateboards or scooters in the shopping mall. As soon as a skateboarder appears, all the adults must go quickly into the stores and stay there until the skateboarder has left.

4 In clothing stores, the sales assistants must let teens try on all the clothes they like. If they don't like the clothes they see in the store window, the sales assistants have to remove them immediately.

5 In music and video game stores, teens are allowed to play with all the games and listen to all the music they want, for as long as they like.

⚠ **ANYONE WHO DOESN'T FOLLOW THESE RULES HAS TO LEARN THEM BY HEART!**

2 **Read the rules again. Mark the sentences T (true) or F (false). Correct the false sentences.**

   1 Teenagers have to behave very well in the shopping mall. ☐

   _____

   2 Teens don't have to pay for snacks and drinks in the cafés. ☐

   _____

   3 Adults must give their seats to teenagers. ☐

   _____

   4 No skateboards are allowed in the shopping mall. ☐

   _____

   5 Young people aren't allowed to touch gaming consoles in the stores. ☐

   _____

   6 If you break the rules, you are not allowed to shop in the shopping mall. ☐

   _____

3 **ANALYZE** **Find four examples of language used to express obligation and permission.**

   _____
   _____
   _____
   _____
   _____
   _____
   _____

 WRITING TIP: rules

- Rules should be short, but clear and easy to understand.
- Use verbs and phrases of obligation and permission.
- Explain exactly what people can or can't do.
- Explain the punishments if you break the rules.
- You can make your set of rules sound funnier if you exaggerate and make them sound particularly strict. For example: *Nobody is allowed to ...,* *Everybody who doesn't follow these rules has to ... .*

4 **PLAN** **You are going to write a set of six rules. These can be serious or light-hearted. Choose ONE of the situations and make a plan. Use the Writing tip to help you.**

- Rules for the swimming pool / gym, or any other place you frequently go to.
- A group of students from another country is going to visit your school. Write the school rules they need to know.
- Rules for your family at home.

5 **PRODUCE** **Write your set of rules in about 200 words. Make sure that it's clear if they're serious or not. Use your plan from Exercise 4.**

 **LISTENING**

1 🔊 **12.02** Listen to the three conversations. Match them with the correct pictures.

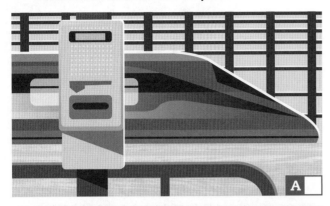

A ☐

B ☐

C ☐

2 🔊 **12.02** Listen again. Write the two important rules in each situation.

Conversation 1

0 *Slow down when you see a sign with three arrows in a circle.*

1 _____

_____

Conversation 2

2 _____

_____

3 _____

_____

Conversation 3

4 _____

_____

5 _____

_____

3 Complete the sentences with the words in the list.

> disagree | referee | ~~sign~~ | slow down
> stamped | ticket

1 When you see the _____*sign*_____ for a traffic circle, you should _____ .

2 You need to put your _____ into a machine and get it _____ .

3 Never argue with the _____ or _____ with the coach.

DIALOGUE

4 🔊 **12.03** Put the conversation in the correct order. Then listen again and check.

☐ **Lexi** Ticket validated? How do I do that?

☐ **Lexi** Sounds easy enough.

☐1 **Lexi** I'm so excited that I'm coming to visit you, but I'm a bit nervous about getting the train from Sistiana to Trieste. Is it very different from getting a train in the US?

☐ **Lexi** OK – that's the same then.

☐ **Alessio** Right. Just don't forget that. Otherwise you'll have to pay a fine.

☐ **Alessio** Not really. The first thing you need to do is get a ticket. You can do that from the ticket window at the station or from a machine.

☐ **Alessio** But – and this is the important thing – you need to get your ticket validated.

☐ **Alessio** Look for a yellow machine, and put your ticket into the machine. It stamps the ticket and that shows the date and the time of day. Now you're ready to go.

Train to TH!NK

Create rules for a new country

5 Imagine a new country has been discovered and you're going to be the ruler of it. Make some notes about your new country. Use these ideas to help you.

- Where is it?
- Who is going to live there?
- What rules do you want to have?

6 Now write six rules for your new country.

_____

_____

_____

_____

_____

_____

_____

_____

_____

_____

 **READING**
Part 6: Open cloze

1 **For each question, write the correct answer. Write one word for each gap.**

HISTORY COMES ALIVE

You can't visit London without a trip to the British Museum. It's one of the most famous museums in the world. The front of the building looks ¹_____ a Greek temple and inside the museum is so enormous that you can't see ²_____ in one day. We decided to visit the Ancient Egyptian collection. The mummies were fascinating, but I'll never forget the senet game. The senet game is a wooden box that has thirty squares on top and the game-pieces inside. This ancient game is ³_____ 1,200 BCE. The rules of senet are still a mystery but we know it was a popular game. Four sets of senet games ⁴_____ even found in the tomb of the boy king Tutankamun!

I think it's really good going to a museum like that: it helps you realise that ancient people weren't as different from us ⁵_____ you might think. They used ⁶_____ enjoy playing games and having fun just as we do. I really learned a lot that day!

EXAM GUIDE: READING PART 6

In B1 Preliminary for Schools Part 6, you have to read a short text and complete the six gaps. You have to think of the words yourself. This is testing grammar knowledge, so the missing words are often auxiliary verbs, prepositions, articles, determiners, common fixed phrases and possessives.

- Read the text to get a general idea of what it's about.
- Read the sentence with the first gap.
- Look carefully at the words <u>before and after</u> the gap as these give you clues about the word you need.
- If you can't think of a word immediately, try to understand the type of word you need, for example verb, article, preposition.
- Try out various possibilities until you find one that sounds best.
- Re-read the text with the new words to check your answers.

CONSOLIDATION

🎧 LISTENING

1 🔊 **12.04** **Listen to the conversation. Circle the correct option: A, B, or C.**

1 What time does the movie start?
  A 7:30
  B 7:40
  C 7:45

2 What type of movie are they going to see?
  A sci-fi movie
  B comedy
  C action movie

3 Why can't they go in to see the movie?
  A They aren't old enough.
  B The movie has already started.
  C You can't enter after eight o'clock.

2 🔊 **12.04** **Listen again and answer the questions.**

0 How did Paul remind Jack about the movie?
  He sent him a text message.

1 Why is Jack a bit late?
  _____

2 What will happen if Jack gets home after 11 p.m.?
  _____

3 What has Jack heard about the movie?
  _____

4 What is the movie called?
  _____

5 What does Jack suggest they do when they can't see the movie?
  _____

🔤 VOCABULARY

3 **Complete the sentences with the words in the list.**

> angry | difference | ~~friends~~ | fun | sure | up

0 We made a lot of new ____*friends*____ on the school trip to Costa Rica.

1 They laughed at my hat! They made _____ of it!

2 Did you make _____ the door was locked before you left the house?

3 I don't believe your story. You made it _____ !

4 Painting the walls has made a big _____ to the room.

5 People dropping trash in the streets makes me really _____ !

4 **Complete the sentences.**

0 They broke a window and got into a lot of t*rouble* with the neighbors.

1 Craig called me and r_____ me to take some music to his party.

2 Of course you're sick – I w_____ you not to drink that old milk.

3 I don't like him much because he m_____ fun of everyone.

4 We trained our dog and now he b_____ very well when we take him out.

5 He really didn't want to come with us at first, but in the end I p_____ him.

6 The teacher was angry with us – she really told us o_____ .

7 I was very surprised to hear that he lost the game – I e_____ him to win.

Ⓖ GRAMMAR

5 **Circle the correct words.**

0 She's such a good actress that they picked *to play* / *her to play* Juliet in *Romeo and Juliet*.

1 If *I'd known* / *I knew* you needed money yesterday, *I'd have lent* / *I lent* you some.

2 My parents always want *that I work* / *me to work* harder at school.

3 **A** Jimmy's coming to the party.
  B Really? Yesterday he said he *isn't* / *wasn't* coming.

4 He said he *didn't see* / *hadn't seen* the movie before, so we went to see it last night.

5 We *would have arrived* / *have arrived* before midnight if we *would have left* / *had left* earlier.

6 **Complete the sentences with the correct form of *let* or *allow*.**

0 Our parents don't _____*let*_____ us play in the yard.

1 At school we aren't _____ to send text messages in class.

2 They didn't _____ me go in to see the movie because I'm too young.

3 She never _____ her friends borrow her things.

4 Are you _____ to wear jeans to school?

5 If I hadn't gotten home on time, my parents wouldn't have _____ me to go out again.

DIALOGUE

7  **12.05** **Complete the conversation with the phrases in the list. There are two phrases you don't need. Then listen and check.**

> check this out | have a word | I'm just saying
> it's not worth it | made fun | make it up
> make sure | playing a joke | ~~was like~~
> We're talking about

Madison You don't look very happy. What's wrong?

Lauren It's James Carter. He makes me so angry! I met him outside school and I said, "Hi James!", and he ⁰ _____*was like*_____ "Wow, Lauren, tell me you didn't pay to have your hair cut like that!"

Madison What? ¹_____ James Carter, right? He's one of the nicest guys at school.

Lauren Madison, I didn't ²_____ . That's exactly what he said. He ³_____ of me in front of my friends!

Madison OK, OK. Don't get angry with me, too! ⁴_____ , he's not usually rude.

Lauren Sorry, yes. It's just that I'm really, really upset!

Madison Look, why don't you calm down and then go and ⁵_____ with him? You know, you can ask him why he said it. And you can ⁶_____ he wasn't just trying to be funny.

Lauren No, I don't want to do that. I could talk to him, but ⁷_____ . He'll only say another mean thing.

Madison OK, it's up to you. Come on, let's go and have lunch.

READING

8 **Read the story and answer the questions.**

0 Why did the writer walk on the beach every day?
Because it helped him to relax and get ideas
for his work.

1 What was the weather like on that morning?
_____

2 What was the little girl in the distance doing?
_____

3 Why was she throwing the starfish into the water?
_____

4 Why did the writer think that she was wasting her time?
_____

5 Why did the girl think that she was making a difference?
_____

STARFISH

There was once a writer who lived close to the ocean. Every morning, he went for a walk along the beach to relax and get ideas before he started work.

One beautiful sunny morning, he saw a little girl in the distance near the water. She was bending down and then standing up – he wasn't sure what she was doing. So he decided to go closer to find out.

When he got near the little girl, he saw that there were a lot of starfish on the beach. The little girl was picking them up, one at a time, and throwing them into the water.

The writer went closer and asked the girl what she was doing. She stopped and looked up at the writer – she seemed surprised. She said that she was throwing the starfish back into the ocean. She said, "If I don't throw the starfish back into the water, they'll die."

Now the writer was surprised. He wanted to persuade her that she was wasting her time. He said, "But look, there are hundreds of starfish here. You can't possibly pick them all up and throw them back. It's not worth it. You can't possibly make a difference here."

The girl looked at him and said nothing. Then she picked up a starfish and threw it into the water. She turned to the writer and said, "If I hadn't thrown it back, it would have died. So I think I made a difference to that one."

WRITING

9 **Write a short story (about 150–200 words), true or made up, that ends with the words *It made a big difference to me*. (Instead of *me*, you could use *him / her / them / us*.)**

PRONUNCIATION

UNIT 1
Sentence stress

1 Complete the sentences with the correct words from the list. (Circle) the stressed word in each sentence.

> great idea | a joke | to be famous one
> changed forever | dangerous places | definitely do
> fantastic time | is for living | car accident
> help you | never heard | the new café

0 That's a _____great idea_____ !
1 Can I _____ ?
2 Then one day, her life _____ .
3 I know. Let's go to _____ !
4 We should _____ it!
5 We had a _____ .
6 She travels to some of the most
   _____ to take photos.
7 They're going _____ day.
8 It was just _____ !
9 Then my aunt had a terrible
   _____ .
10 I've _____ him complain.
11 "Life _____," she said.

2 🔊 1.02 Listen, check, and repeat.

UNIT 2
Word stress

1 Write the verbs from the list in the correct columns.

> believe | concentrate | forget | guess | know
> recognize | remember | suppose | think

1	One syllable	2	Two syllables	3	Three syllables
	_____		_____		_concentrate_
	_____		_____		_____
	_____		_____		_____

2 🔊 2.01 Listen, check, and repeat.

3 Which syllable is stressed? Write the verbs in the correct columns.

> believe | concentrate | consider | discuss
> explain | imagine | listen | motivate
> recognize | remember | study | wonder

Oo	oO	Ooo	oOo
_____	_believe_	_____	_____
_____	_____	_____	_____
_____	_____	_____	_____

4 🔊 2.02 Listen, check, and repeat.

UNIT 3
Words ending in /ər/

1 Complete the sentences with the comparative forms of the adjectives in the list.

> early | funny | good | old
> quiet | slow | tall | clean

0 My sister's a lot _____cleaner_____ than me. Her bedroom is always clean.
1 There's too much noise here – let's go somewhere _____ .
2 He's very smart and much _____ at math than me.
3 Mom has to go to work at eight o'clock; she gets up _____ than the rest of us.
4 My brother's 1.72 meters. He's _____ than me.
5 Jake's fourteen and his sister's ten. He's _____ than her.
6 You're driving too fast. Could you please go a little _____ ?
7 This comedy show is much _____ than the one we saw last week.

2 🔊 3.01 Listen, check, and repeat.

3 Write the comparatives from Exercise 1 in the correct columns. <u>Underline</u> the stressed syllable. Remember that the final syllable "er" is never stressed. It has the /ər/ sound.

Two syllables	Three syllables
better	*earlier*

4 🔊 **3.02** Listen, check, and repeat.

UNIT 4
The short /ʌ/ vowel sound

1 Circle the word in each line that doesn't have the /ʌ/ sound (e.g., the sound in *son*, *one*, and *done*).

	A	B	C	D
0	son	one	done	(dog)
1	fun	won	home	come
2	shout	young	much	tongue
3	enough	cousin	you	love
4	must	mother	nose	doesn't
5	trouble	jump	other	note
6	love	stuff	funny	ground
7	put	wonder	under	nothing
8	could	some	lovely	brother
9	Sunday	Monday	over	cover
10	none	use	monkey	another
11	good	blood	touch	couple

2 🔊 **4.01** Listen, check, and repeat.

UNIT 5
The /ɑ/ vowel sound (spelled with o)

1 Match the statements (1–6) with the responses (a–g).

0	Has Tom ever been to Boston?	*e*
1	I thought you went to the coffee shop.	_____
2	What's wrong? You look sick.	_____
3	Please stop by the office on Monday.	_____
4	Are you too hot? Your face is so red!	_____
5	How long has it been since you saw John?	_____
6	Tonya and Ron look tired.	_____

a I know. I'm going to the doctor.
b No, I got lost.
c A long time – since October.
d They were playing soccer.
e Yes, he has. He's gone there every summer since he was ten.
f I got a sunburn. I forgot my sunscreen.
g I can come on Tuesday.

2 🔊 **5.01** Listen, check, and repeat.

3 Circle the words with the /ɑ/ sound (spelled with o).

4 🔊 **5.01** Listen again, check, and repeat.

UNIT 6
/f/, /v/, and /b/ consonant sounds

1 🔊 **6.01** Listen and circle the word you hear.

	a	b		a	b
0	(few)	view	**3**	ferry	very
1	fast	vast	**4**	leaf	leave
2	fan	van	**5**	off	of

2 🔊 **6.01** Listen again, check, and repeat.

3 Circle the correct words to complete the sentences.

0 They went out in Bill's dad's (boat) / vote.
1 That's a *berry* / *very* good idea.
2 She wants to be a *vet* / *bet* when she's older.
3 I wore my *best* / *vest* clothes to the party.
4 He drives a white *van* / *ban* for his job.

4 🔊 **6.02** Listen, check, and repeat.

UNIT 7
Intonation in question tags

1 🔊 7.01 **Listen and draw ↗ when the voice goes up and ↘ when the voice goes down.**

Example 1: Your name's Lisa, isn't it? ↗
Example 2: You like chocolate, don't you? ↘

1 Tony hasn't been hurt, has he?
2 Helen's in your sister's class, isn't she?
3 I don't have any money, do I?
4 That's not the right answer, is it?
5 You're Julie's cousin, aren't you?

2 🔊 7.01 **Listen again and check.**

3 **Check (✓) the correct explanation (A or B) for each tag from Exercise 1.**

   Example 1
   A I've met Lisa before. ✓
   B I'm not sure what this girl's name is. ☐

   Example 2
   A I'm surprised because you don't want any chocolate. ☐
   B I know you like chocolate. ✓

   1 A I know Tony hasn't been to Africa. ☐
     B I'm surprised that Tony's been to Africa. ☐
   2 A I think Helen's in your sister's class. ☐
     B I don't know if Helen's in your sister's class. ☐
   3 A I don't know if I have money or not. ☐
     B I know I don't have any money. ☐
   4 A I don't know if that's the right answer. ☐
     B I know that isn't the right answer. ☐
   5 A I don't know Julie. ☐
     B I think you are Julie's cousin. ☐

4 🔊 7.01 **Listen again, check, and repeat.**

UNIT 8
The /juː/ sound

1 **Find the words with the /juː/ sound. There are nine words in total and they all appear in Unit 8.**

U	E	U	R	E	K	A	E	C	A
S	Q	E	W	T	O	N	W	O	U
E	F	E	E	O	T	M	H	M	S
D	Z	R	W	R	C	U	O	P	U
I	A	O	W	T	R	U	R	U	A
I	F	U	T	U	R	E	R	T	L
Y	O	U	C	H	R	F	U	E	L
R	E	V	I	E	W	T	U	R	Y

2 🔊 8.01 **Listen and check.**

3 **Circle the word that doesn't have the /juː/ sound.**
   0 university (flew) nephew
   1 music computer umbrella
   2 view guess few
   3 future threw review
   4 amusing butter useful

4 🔊 8.02 **Listen, check, and repeat.**

UNIT 9
/tʃ/ and /dʒ/ consonant sounds

1 **Complete the sentences with the correct word from the list below.**

   | ~~chair~~ | charities | future | match | switch |

   0 When she broke her leg, she had to use a wheel___*chair*___ .
   1 Did you see the tennis championship? It was an exciting _____ .
   2 I'd like to travel the world in the _____ .
   3 When she was younger, she worked as a _____board operator.
   4 There are many _____ to help children in need.

2 **Which one sound occurs in all of the words in the list in Exercise 1? Circle the sound in each word.**

3 🔊 9.03 **Check your answer with the key. Then listen and repeat.**

4 **Complete the sentences with the correct word from the list.**

   | bridge | ~~changing~~ | join | jokes | message |

   0 Many jobs are disappearing because the world is ___*changing*___ so fast.
   1 We're going to the new café. Would you like to _____ us?
   2 We have to cross that _____ to go over the river.
   3 My best friend makes me laugh. She's always telling _____ .
   4 If you can't come, just send me a text _____ .

5 **Which one sound occurs in all of the words in the list in Exercise 4? Circle the sound in each word.**

6 🔊 9.04 **Check your answer with the key. Then listen and repeat.**

UNIT 10
/tʃ/ and /ʃ/ consonant sounds

1 🔊 **10.02** **Who do you meet? Put your finger on *Start*. Listen to the words. Go up if you hear the /tʃ/ sound (e.g., <u>ch</u>ips) and down if you hear the /ʃ/ sound (e.g., <u>sh</u>ips). Say the word at the end.**

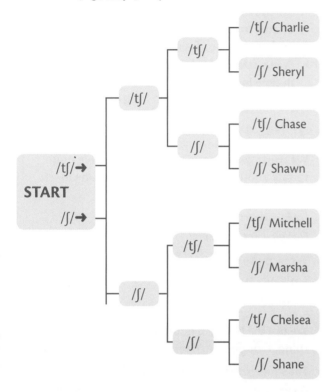

0 <u>sh</u>oes – <u>ch</u>eese – wi<u>sh</u>. Who do you meet? <u>*Marsha*</u>
1 _____ **2** _____ **3** _____ **4** _____ **5** _____

2 🔊 **10.02** **Listen again, check, and repeat.**

3 🔊 **10.03** **Complete the sentences with the different spellings of the /ʃ/ sound. Listen and check.**

0 My sister loves fa_<u>sh</u>_ion magazines.
1 I put my money in the ma____ine, but it didn't give me a can of soda!
2 I wi____ I had a lot of money so I could buy that bike.
3 We're going to the beach now. Are you ____ure you don't want to come?
4 We can get all the informa____ion we need at the train station.

4 🔊 **10.03** **Check your answers with the key. Then listen and repeat.**

5 🔊 **10.04** **Write the words on the correct line. Then listen and check.**

> competi<u>t</u>ion | conclu<u>s</u>ion | deci<u>s</u>ion | deli<u>c</u>ious
> ~~fu<u>t</u>ure~~ | mix<u>t</u>ure | pa<u>ss</u>ion | ques<u>t</u>ion | revi<u>s</u>ion

/ʃ/ – fashion _____ _____ _____
/tʃ/ – picture _*future*_ _____ _____
/ʒ/ – television _____ _____ _____

UNIT 11
Polite intonation

1 **Where would you hear each of these statements or questions? Write A for airport, R for restaurant, or C for classroom.**

2 🔊 **11.01** **Listen and put a checkmark (✓) if the speaker sounds polite. Put an X if the speaker sounds rude.**

		Where?	Is it polite?
0	Put that suitcase over there.	A	X
1	When does the plane leave?		
2	I don't understand the question, Mr. Jones.		
3	Are you ready to order?		
4	Raise your hand if you know the answer.		
5	You arrive in London at eight thirty.		
6	Do you have anything without cheese?		

3 🔊 **11.01** **Listen again, check, and repeat.**

4 🔊 **11.02** **Now the sentences are said politely. How is the speaker's voice different? Listen and repeat.**

UNIT 12
Silent consonants

1 <u>Underline</u> **the spelling mistakes. Write the correct spelling.**

0 That's the <u>rong</u> answer to this question. _<u>*wrong*</u>_
1 Her dauter's six and her name's Cynthia.
2 We played rock, paper, sissors in class yesterday.
3 Woud you like a drink of water?
4 My parents are taking me to an iland on our next vacation.
5 Our English class is an our long on Fridays.
6 I'm going to order the samon and salad. It looks good!
7 I asked her if she was OK, but she didn't anser me.
8 We musn't leave the classroom before the bell rings.

2 🔊 **12.01** **Listen and repeat.**

GRAMMAR REFERENCE

UNIT 1
Present perfect with *just*, *already*, and *yet*

We often use the present perfect with the words *just / already / yet*.

1   We use *just* before the past participle to say that something happened a short time ago.

   *They've **just** come back from their trip.*

2   We use *already* at the end of a sentence or before the past participle to show surprise, or to emphasize that something has been done, or finished, sooner than expected.

   *Have you finished **already**?*
   *No food, thanks – I've **already** eaten.*

3   We use *yet* at the end of negative sentences and questions to emphasise that something hasn't happened but probably will in the future.

   *Have you finished your homework **yet**?*
   *I haven't played that game **yet** (but I will).*

Present perfect vs. simple past

1   We use the simple past to talk about events that are complete and finished, or "before now," at the time of speaking.

   *I **saw** you in town yesterday. Who **were** you with?*

2   We use the present perfect to connect the past and "now" (at the time of speaking).

   *I **haven't seen** you this week. Where **have you been**?*

UNIT 2
Present perfect with *for* and *since*

1   We can use the present perfect to talk about something that began in the past and continues to be true in the present.

   *We**'ve lived** here for ten years. (= and we still live here)*
   *She**'s played** in a band since 2018. (= and she still plays in it)*

2   We talk about the time between when something started and now with *for* or *since*.

   • We use the word *for* when we mention a period of time from the past until now.
     for half an hour / for three months / for a long time
   • We use the word *since* when we mention a point in time in the past.
     since six o'clock / since 2012 / since last weekend

a, an, the, or no article

1   We use *a, an* before a singular, countable noun to talk about something for the first time in a conversation.

   *Look – there's **a horse** in the yard!*
   *Do you want **an apple**?*

   We also use *a / an* when we are not talking about a specific thing.

   *I don't have **a** computer.*

2   We use *the* before a noun when it is clear which thing(s) or person/people we are talking about.

   ***The** strawberries in our garden are delicious.*
   *Do you have **the** book? (= the book we were talking about before)*
   ***The** woman next door is really friendly.*

   We also use *the* when there is only one thing that exists.

   *Look at **the** moon!*

3   We use no article (zero article) before plural countable nouns, and before uncountable nouns, when we are talking about things in general.

   ***Cars** are expensive.*
   ***Love** is the most important thing.*

UNIT 3
Comparative and superlative adjectives (review)

1   When we want to compare two things, or two groups of things, we use a comparative form + *than*.

   *My sister is **older than** me.*
   *My old phone was **more expensive than** my new one.*
   *The movie is **better than** the book.*

2 With short adjectives, we normally add *-er*. With longer adjectives (more than two syllables), we normally don't change the adjective – we put *more* in front of it.

hot ➔ hot**ter**   short ➔ short**er**   smart ➔ smart**er**

interesting ➔ **more** interesting   exciting ➔ **more** exciting

3 Some adjectives are irregular – they have a different comparative form.

good ➔ better   bad ➔ worse   far ➔ further

(not) as … as

When we want to say that two things are the same (or not the same) we can use *(not) as* + adjective + *as*.

She's **as tall as** her mother now.

This question is**n't as easy as** the last one.

Making a comparison stronger or weaker

We can make a comparison stronger or weaker by using *much / far, a lot,* or *a little / a bit*. These words come before the comparison.

His computer is **far better** than mine.

His bike was **much more expensive** than mine.

He lives **a little further** from school than I do.

Adverbs and comparative adverbs

1 We use adverbs to describe verbs — they say how an action is or was performed.

She <u>shouted</u> **angrily**.   <u>Run</u> **quickly**!

They <u>got</u> to the concert **early**.

We can also use adverbs before adjectives.

It was **really** <u>cold</u> on Sunday.

The coffee was **incredibly** <u>hot</u>, so I couldn't drink it.

2 Most adverbs are formed by adjective + *-ly*.

slow ➔ slow**ly**   nice ➔ nice**ly**

If the adjective ends in *-le*, we drop the *-e* and add *-y*.

incredible ➔ incredib**ly**   possible ➔ possib**ly**

If the adjective ends in consonant + *-y*, we change the *-y* to *-i* and add *-ly*.

angry ➔ angr**ily**   lucky ➔ luck**ily**   hungry ➔ hungr**ily**

3 Some adverbs are irregular – they don't have an *-ly* ending.

good ➔ well   fast ➔ fast   hard ➔ hard

early ➔ early   late ➔ late

4 To compare adverbs, we use the same rules as we do when we compare adjectives. With short adverbs, we add *-er* or *-r* and *than* after the adverb.

I worked **hard**, but Sue worked **harder than** me!

5 With longer adverbs, we use *more* (+ adverb) + *than*.

She does things **more easily than** me.

6 To compare the adverb *well*, we use *better … than*. To compare the adverb *far*, we use *further … than*.

He cooks **better than** me.

London to Mumbai is **further than** London to New York.

UNIT 4
Indefinite pronouns

1 We can use the words *every / some / no / any* together with *one / thing / where* to make compound nouns.

everyone = all the people

everything = all the things

everywhere = all the places

someone = a person, but we don't know who

something = a thing, but we don't know which

somewhere = a place, but we don't know where

no one = none of the people

nothing = none of the things

nowhere = none of the places

anyone = any person / any of the people

anything = any of the things

anywhere = any of the places

2 These words are all singular.

Something smells nice. **No one's** here. **Nothing was** found. **Everywhere was** full. **Someone has** opened my desk.

3 We don't use negatives with *nothing* and *no one*. We use *anything* or *anyone* instead.

I don't know **anyone** here.

(NOT I ~~don't know no one~~ here.)

all (some / none / any) of them

With other nouns and pronouns, we *use all of / some of / none of* + plural or uncountable noun/pronoun.

All of them are yours.   **Some of** the teachers are really nice.

None of my friends called me yesterday.

Do **any of** you know the answer?

should(n't), had better, ought to

1 *Should, had ('d) better,* and *ought to* are all used to give advice.

2 *Should* and *ought to* both mean "I think it's (not) a good idea for you/me/him (etc.) to do this."

You **should get** more exercise. (= I think it is a good idea for you to get more exercise.)

She **shouldn't talk** in class. (= I think it is not a good idea for her to talk in class.)

We **ought to** leave now. (= I think it is a good idea for us to leave now.)

3 The meaning of *had better* is often stronger. The speaker wants to say that there are negative consequences if the person ignores the advice.

*I'd **better run**. (or I'll be late)*
*You'd **better not talk** in class. (or the teacher will be angry)*

4 *Should, had better,* and *ought to* are all followed by the infinitive of another verb.

*You **should be** more careful.*
*I **ought to eat** more fruit.*
*We'd **better hurry** or we'll be late.*

5 *Should* and *had better* form the negative by adding *not* afterwards.

*They **shouldn't** be so rude.*
*We'd **better not** stay out late.*

We make *ought to* negative by putting *not* after *ought* (but we don't use this form very often).

*You **ought not to** make so much noise.*

UNIT 5
Present perfect continuous

1 The present perfect continuous is formed with the present tense of *have* + *been* + the *-ing* form of the verb.

*I've **been reading** since breakfast.*
***Have** you **been sitting** here all day?*

2 Sentences with the present perfect always connect the present and the past. We often use the present perfect continuous to talk about activities that started in the past and are still continuing now.

*She's **been running** for an hour. (= She started running an hour ago, and she is still running.)*

3 We also use the present perfect continuous to talk about actions with a result in the present. These actions may or may not be complete.

*I'm tired because I've **been working**.*
*Jack's feeling sick because he **hasn't been eating** well.*

4 We also use the present perfect continuous to talk about actions that began in the past and continue to the present, but perhaps we are not doing the action at the time of speaking.

*We've **been studying** Spanish for six months. (= We started studying six months ago and we are still studying, but we're not studying at this exact moment.)*

Present perfect vs. present perfect continuous

1 We use the present perfect to show that an action is finished or to focus on what (and how much) we have completed in a period of time.

*I've **written** an email.*
*I've **written** twelve emails this morning.*

2 We use the present perfect continuous to show that an action is still going on or to focus on how long something has been in progress.

*I've **been reading** this book for two days.*
*I've **been reading** detective stories for years.*

Compare the sentences:

*She's **been writing** books for many years.*
*She's **written** over twenty books.*

UNIT 6
will (not), may (not), might (not) for prediction

1 We can use the modal verb *will* (*'ll*) or *will not* (*won't*) to make predictions about the future.

*Don't worry about the exam – it **won't be** difficult.*

2 We use *might/might not* or *may/may not* to make less certain predictions about the future.

*It **might rain** this afternoon – if it does, then I **may not** go the match.*

First conditional / unless in first conditional sentences

1 We use the first conditional to talk about possible actions / situations in the future and their (possible) results.

If I finish my homework, I'll go out.

2 We often make conditional sentences by using *if* + subject + simple present in the *if* clause and *will/ won't / might/might not* in the main clause.

*If I **have** time this afternoon, I'll **go** for a walk.*
*We **might go** out tonight if there's nothing good on TV.*

3 We can also use the word *unless* in conditional sentences – it means *if not*.

*She **won't come unless** you ask her. (= She won't come if you don't ask her.)*

4 There are two clauses in these sentences. We can put the main clause first or the *if/unless* clause first. When the *if/unless* clause comes first, there is *a comma (,) after it*.

***Unless** you tell me, I won't know what to do.*
*I won't know what to do **unless** you tell me.*

UNIT 7
Future forms (review)

1   We often use the simple present to talk about fixed future events.

*My uncle is coming to visit us. His plane **arrives** at six o'clock tomorrow.*

2   We often use *be going to* to talk about future plans and intentions.

*I'**m going to be** a doctor when I grow up.*

3   We often use *will/won't* to make predictions about the future.

*Don't worry about her. I'm sure she'**ll be** OK.*

4   We often use the present continuous to talk about future arrangements.

*They'**re getting** married next June.*

Question tags

1   Question tags are positive or negative questions at the end of statements. We add "tags" to the end of statements:

a)   when we are not sure that what we are saying is correct, and we want the other person to say if we are correct or not.

b)   when we are sure that what we are saying is correct and we want the other person to say something about it.

2   Tags in (a) above have a rising intonation pattern.

➚

A: *You're Spanish, aren't you?*
B: *No, I'm not. I'm Mexican.*

Tags in (b) above have a falling intonation pattern.

➘

A: *You're Spanish, aren't you?*
B: *That's right. I'm from Barcelona.*

3   With positive statements, we usually use a negative question tag.

*I'<u>m</u> early, **aren't I**?   He'<u>s</u> very friendly, **isn't he**?*

With negative statements, we usually use a positive question tag.

*It <u>isn't difficult</u>, **is it**?   She <u>doesn't like</u> dogs, **does she**?*

4   With *be*, modal verbs (*can, must, should, will, might*, etc.), *have got*, and the present perfect, we repeat the auxiliary verb in the tag.

*They <u>aren't</u> from here, **are they**?*
*You'<u>ll</u> come to my party, **won't you**?*
*We <u>don't have</u> any milk, **do we**?*
*They'<u>ve gone</u> away on vacation, **haven't they**?*

5   With all other verbs, we use *do / don't / does / doesn't* (simple present) or *did / didn't* (simple past).

*You <u>love</u> this song, **don't you**?*
*I <u>gave</u> it back to you, **didn't I**?*

nor / neither / so

1   When someone says something and we want to agree with it, we can use *so / nor* (or *neither*) + auxiliary verb + *I*.

I am really happy.	***So am I.***
I don't like cold showers.	***Nor (Neither) do I.***

2   We use *so* to agree with a positive statement or idea and *nor* (or *neither*) to agree with a negative statement or idea.

*I **was** tired yesterday.*	*So was I.*
*I **didn't enjoy** the movie.*	***Nor (Neither)** did I.*

3   Notice that the auxiliary we use after *so / nor / neither* depends on what the other person says.

*I **can't** sing.*	*Neither **can** I.*
*I'**ve been** to Paris.*	*So **have** I.*

UNIT 8
Simple past vs. past continuous (review)

1   When we talk about the past, we use the simple past for actions that happened at one particular time. We use the past continuous for background actions.

*When Steve **called** me, I **was reading** a book.*
*Who **scored** the goal? I **wasn't watching**.*

2   We often use *when* followed by the simple past and *while* followed by the past continuous.

*She was swimming **when** the shark **attacked**.*
***While** I **was studying** for the test, I fell asleep.*

used to

1   We can use *used to* when we want to talk about an action that happened regularly in the past, but that doesn't happen any more.

*My mother **used to work** in a bank. (= My mother worked in a bank in the past, but she doesn't any more.)*

2   *used to* is followed by the base form of the main verb.

*Our team used to **be** much better than it is now.*

3   The negative of *used to* is *didn't use to*.

*I **didn't use to like** rap music. (= In the past, I didn't like rap music, but now I like it.)*

We make questions with *used to* using *Did + subject + use to ...?*

***Did** you **use to go** to school in Leeds?*

Second conditional

1   We use the second conditional to talk about unreal or imagined situations in the present or future.

*If I **was** good at tennis, I **would play** for the school team. (= I am not good at tennis and don't play for the school team.)*

*She **wouldn't be** in the photography class if she **wasn't** interested in it. (= She is here because she is interested in it.)*

2   The second conditional has two parts (or "clauses"). We usually make the second conditional like this:

If clause	Main clause
if + simple past + comma	would/wouldn't + main verb
If I **lived** in town,	I**'d go** to the movies more often.
If he **was** nicer,	more people **would talk** to him.

We can change the order of the two clauses if we want to. When we put the *if* clause first, we write a comma (,) after it. If we put the main clause first, there is no comma.

*I **would go** to the movies more often if I **lived** in town.*
*More people **would talk** to him if he **was** nicer.*

3   The word *would* is often spoken as *'d*. We can write it like this in informal writing, too. Also, *would not* is often spoken as *wouldn't*.

I wish

When we want to talk about how we would like something in the present to be different, we can use *I wish* + past tense.

*I wish you **were** here. (= You are not here and I am not happy about it.)*

*I wish we **could go** out tonight. (= We can not go out tonight and I am not happy about it.)*

*I wish it **wasn't** raining today. (= It is raining today and I am not happy about it.)*

UNIT 9
The passive (simple present, simple past, present continuous, present perfect)

1   We use the passive when it isn't important who does the action or when we don't know who does it. The passive is also used when the action is more important than who does/did it.

*These cars **are made** in Japan. (It isn't important who makes them.)*
*This house **was built** in 1895. (We don't know who built it.)*

2   The passive is formed with the verb *be* + the past participle of a verb. The verb *be* can be in any tense.

Simple present passive:
*These watches **are sold** all over the world.*
Present continuous passive:
*I think **we are being watched**.*
Simple past passive:
*The city **was destroyed** in an earthquake.*
Present perfect passive:
*An important decision **has been made** today.*

UNIT 10
Past perfect

1   We use the past perfect when we need to make it clear that one action happened *before* another action in the past.

*When we got to the theater, the play **had started**.*
(= The play started before we got to the theater.)

Compare this with:

*When we got to the theater, the play **started**.*
(= The play started when/after we got to the theater.)

2   We form the past perfect with *had ('d)* / *had not (hadn't)* + the past participle of the main verb.

*She didn't watch the movie because she **had seen** it.*

Past perfect continuous

1   We use the past perfect continuous to talk about situations or activities that started in the past and were still continuing at another time in the past.

*She was very tired because she **had been working** for a very long time.*
*When he got there, she **had been waiting** for an hour.*

2   We form the past perfect continuous with the past perfect of the verb *to be (had (not) been)* + the *-ing* form of the main verb.

*I didn't know the answer to the question because I **hadn't been listening**.*

3   The past perfect continuous focuses on how long an activity had been happening. It talks about situations or activities that may have stopped and may have had a result in the past.

*The ground was very wet because it **had been raining** all night.*
*We were tired because we**'d been traveling** since the day before.*

UNIT 11
Reported statements

1   When we report what someone said in the past, we use reported speech. In reported speech, we often use the verb *said* or *told (me)*.

"The music's terrible," my friend said. → *My friend **said** the music was terrible.*

2   We can use the word *that* between *said* or *told (me)* and the rest of the sentence, or we can leave it out.

*I **said that** I wasn't hungry.* OR *I **said** I wasn't hungry.*

3   We often change the verb tense between direct speech and reported speech, like this:

Direct speech	Reported speech
Present (simple/continuous)	→ Past (simple/continuous)
Past (simple/continuous)	→ Past perfect (simple/continuous)
Present perfect	→ Past perfect
am/is/are going to	→ *was/were going to*
can/can't	→ *could/couldn't*
will/won't	→ *would/wouldn't*

Verb patterns

1   A common structure in English is verb + personal noun/pronoun + *to* infinitive.

*I **want you to stay**.* (NOT: *I want that you stay.*)
*He **asked Sarah to help** him.* (NOT: *He asked that Sarah helped him.*)

2   There are many verbs that follow this structure. (See Student's Book Unit 11 page 107)

*He **told us to be** quiet.*
*My parents **encouraged my brother to go** to college.*
*They **warned us not to go** in.*
*He **reminded the children not to be** late.*

UNIT 12
be allowed to / let

1   We use *be allowed to* to say that you do (or don't) have permission to do something. It is a passive construction: it is not important who gives (or doesn't give) the permission.

*At my school, we **are allowed to** wear sneakers.*
*You **aren't allowed to** bike here.*

2   We use *let* to say that someone gives you, or doesn't give you, permission to do something. It is an active construction.

*I **let** my brother borrow my tablet sometimes.*
*Our teacher **didn't let** us use dictionaries for the test.*

3   With *let*, the structure is *let* + person + infinitive without *to*.

*She **didn't let me answer** the question.*
*I'm not going to **let you borrow** my pen.*

4   With *be allowed to*, the structure is person + the correct form of *be* + *allowed* + *to* infinitive.

*You **aren't allowed to leave** your bikes here.*

Third conditional

1   We use the third conditional to talk about unreal, imaginary situations in the past and their imagined results.

If you had practiced, you wouldn't have lost.
(= You <u>didn't practice</u>, and you <u>lost</u>.)

2   The third conditional has two parts (or clauses). We usually make the third conditional like this:

If clause	Main clause
If + past perfect	*would have / wouldn't have* + main verb
*If my sister **had asked** me,*	*I'd have told** her.*
*If I'd **heard** the alarm clock,*	*I **wouldn't have been** late.*

3   We can change the order of the two clauses if we want to.

*I **would have told** my sister if she'd **asked** me.*
*I **wouldn't have been** late if I'd **heard** the alarm clock.*

4   When we put the *if* clause first, we write a comma (,) after it. When we put the main clause first, there is no comma.

IRREGULAR VERBS

Base form	Simple past	Past participle
be	was / were	been
beat	beat	beaten
become	became	become
begin	began	begun
break	broke	broken
bring	brought	brought
build	built	built
buy	bought	bought
can	could	–
catch	caught	caught
choose	chose	chosen
come	came	come
cost	cost	cost
cut	cut	cut
do	did	done
draw	drew	drawn
drink	drank	drunk
drive	drove	driven
eat	ate	eaten
fall	fell	fallen
feel	felt	felt
fight	fought	fought
find	found	found
fly	flew	flown
forget	forgot	forgotten
get	got	gotten
give	gave	given
go	went	gone
grow	grew	grown
hang	hung	hung
have	had	had
hear	heard	heard
hit	hit	hit
hold	held	held
hurt	hurt	hurt
keep	kept	kept
know	knew	known
lead	led	led

Base form	Simple past	Past participle
leave	left	left
lend	lent	lent
let	let	let
lie	lay	lain
light	lit	lit
lose	lost	lost
make	made	made
mean	meant	meant
meet	met	met
pay	paid	paid
put	put	put
read /riːd/	read /red/	read /red/
ride	rode	ridden
ring	rang	rung
rise	rose	risen
run	ran	run
say	said	said
see	saw	seen
sell	sold	sold
send	sent	sent
set	set	set
shoot	shot	shot
show	showed	shown
sing	sang	sung
sit	sat	sat
sleep	slept	slept
speak	spoke	spoken
spend	spent	spent
stand	stood	stood
steal	stole	stolen
strike	struck	struck
swim	swam	swum
take	took	taken
teach	taught	taught
tell	told	told
think	thought	thought
throw	threw	thrown
understand	understood	understood
wake	woke	woken
wear	wore	worn
win	won	won
write	wrote	written